LB
2165
.V54
1990

S0-AYT-213

A VIEW FROM THE TOP

Liberal Arts Presidents on Teacher Education

Thomas Warren, Editor
Beloit College

Association of
Independent Liberal Arts Colleges
for Teacher Education
and University Press of America

UNIVERSITY
PRESS OF
AMERICA

GOSHEN COLLEGE LIBRARY
GOSHEN, INDIANA

Lanham • New York • London

Copyright © 1990 by

University Press of America®, Inc.
4720 Boston Way
Lanham, Maryland 20706

3 Henrietta Street
London WC2E 8LU England

All rights reserved
Printed in the United States of America
British Cataloging in Publication Information Available

"Ornaments of Society" ©1990 by John H. Jacobson

Library of Congress Cataloging-in-Publication Data

A View from the top : liberal arts presidents on teacher
education / Thomas Warren, editor.
        p.   cm.
1. Teachers—Training of—United States.
2. Education, Humanistic—United States.
I. Warren, Thomas, 1939– .   II. Association of
Independent Liberal Arts Colleges for Teacher Education.
LB2165.V54   1990   370'.71'0973—dc20   90–44787 CIP

ISBN 0–8191–7980–9 (alk. paper)
ISBN 0-8191-7981-7 (pbk. : alk. paper)

 The paper used in this publication meets the minimum requirements of
American National Standard for Information Sciences—Permanence
of Paper for Printed Library Materials, ANSI Z39.48–1984.

Contents

Foreword

The Association of Liberal Arts Colleges for Teacher Education exists as a voice for teacher education in liberal arts settings. We have a responsibility to speak internally to our own administrators and faculty as well as externally to those who do not know us well. Our publications efforts are designed to meet these goals.

This first effort in a projected series of monographs is entitled *A View from the Top* and presents articles by several of our presidents and others. Some of their voices reflect the ideals and values of their respective institutions. Others share experiences that have proven successful in these special settings. Still others are hardnosed and pragmatic in discussing teacher preparation as well as education in the wider world.

All recognize the importance of several elements in providing quality education. These include the importance of a liberal education, the value of mentoring by faculty who like teaching and show it, the sense of community that exists in independent liberal arts colleges, and the importance of a sense of mission in teacher education.

It is our hope that this monograph will inspire readers to examine their own institutions critically and to speak out loudly and clearly about the values that guide and strengthen teacher education.

Ann Converse Shelly
President, AILACTE
1989– 1990

Foreword

From a College President ...

Your critics will be looking to learn whether you put your ambition, your energy and your education in the service of choices that confirm their darkest suspicions. They will be looking to learn whether you choose, in the poet Philip Larkin's words, merely to "listen to money singing." Larkin wrote:

> I listen to money singing. It's like looking down
> From long french windows at a provincial town,
> The slums, the canal, the churches ornate and mad
> In the evening sun. It is intensely sad

None of us who know you well believes that you will, in fact, claim your adulthood by the intensely sad and profoundly banal act of choosing to "listen to money singing." You have the opportunity to confound your critics by making choices worthy of your talents and your idealism; choices that will make the common good your own. I should like to suggest to you one such choice. I would have you, as citizens, support in every possible way excellence in elementary and secondary school teaching.

In perhaps the finest autobiography by an American, Henry Adams deliberated upon the nature and purposes of education. In one of his noblest sentences, he celebrated the importance of the teacher: "A teacher affects eternity; he can never tell where his influence stops."

Adams may have tested the limits of metaphor when he linked teachers to eternity, but he got it right in characterizing the influence of teachers. Teachers—like parents—form our minds, enlarge our vision, and elevate our aspirations. By emphasizing that literacy and learning are the very foundations of a democratic republic, teachers prepare men and women, of all races and circumstances, to exercise the responsibilities of citizenship. By educating us to deal with words, with symbols, with values, and with people, teachers superintend our intellectual and moral development and extend our capacity to lead humane and fruitful lives. More than any other persons in society, teachers are the curators of our heritage.

Because the function of teachers is so fundamentally important, one of the great unfinished items on the agenda of this nation is to strengthen the quality of teaching at all levels of education, and most especially in elementary and secondary schools. We need teachers who can, by the model of their mastery and the glow of their enthusiasm, capture the minds and imaginations of students—teachers who can motivate students to pursue their studies with vigor and excitement, teachers who can animate their students to achieve, with assurance and satisfaction, their individual destinies. The challenge is an immense and momentous one. . . .

Until we are prepared to support teachers adequately, to grant them the esteem they merit, and in every way to demonstrate that we appreciate the crucial importance of their calling we will not attract to our elementary and secondary schools teachers of the quality we need to educate the informed citizens, inspired leaders, and skilled professionals that our nation most certainly requires. . . .

By assuming responsibility to defend the indispensability of learning, by summoning the clarity of purpose to help our society make teaching the most satisfying and respected of professions, you will define yourselves as a generation with a cause.

And because the public consequences of this cause will extend well beyond the present moment, to the time of your children and your grandchildren, you may even, as Henry Adams put it, help to affect eternity. That would be no small achievement for a college generation that commenced upon its adulthood under an indictment that it wanted little more than to "listen to money singing."

James O. Freeman
President of Dartmouth College
From his Commencement Address of
June 11, 1989

vii

Preface

Elephants, Mice, and Presidents

L iberal arts colleges that educate teachers have an opportunity to make substantial new contributions as the decade of the 1990s unfolds. These independent, diverse institutions embody traditions and programs which respond well to the criticisms and challenges to teacher education that began receiving public attention several years ago and that will reach a new intensity as teacher shortages grow. The time is right for liberal arts colleges to play a larger role in educating the bright creative teaching force that this country needs to replace teachers who will be retiring soon in unprecedented numbers.

One dimension of this opportunity involves publicizing what liberal arts colleges stand for and accomplish in teacher education both at individual campuses and on a larger scale. It is no exaggeration to say that liberal arts colleges have, in effect, hidden their teacher education program lamps under bushel baskets for years. Too many people assume that teacher education is the exclusive business of large research universities or teacher training colleges turned "universities."

Minimal publicity for independent liberal arts colleges that educate teachers has been partly due to the lack of a national organization prior to 1980. The formation of the Association of Independent Liberal Arts Colleges of Teacher Education (AILACTE) in that year did much to bring together many institutions and articulate common interests. However, in the early years of the 1980s the small AILACTE voice was no match for that of public university-dominated organizations such as The Association of Colleges and Schools of Education in State Universities and Land Grant Colleges and Affiliated Private Universities, Teacher Education Council of the State Colleges and Universities, or the American Association of Colleges of Teacher Education (AACTE) to which AILACTE retains a "fraternal" affiliation. These groups and the institutions that dominate them have spoken for their brand of teacher education far out of proportion to their numbers. The interests of independent institutions, especially small ones, often have been benignly overlooked or only incidentally addressed.

Joseph Stoltzfus, President of Goshen College, summarizes this state of affairs succinctly when he says, "While the Holmes Group seems intent on teaching the elephantine schools of education new tricks, the group overlooks completely the fact that the mouse at the elephant's feet might be a better teacher than another elephant."

In recent years AILACTE's influence, while still not proportional to the number of its institutions, has increased on several fronts: (1) The Association's members are much better represented on boards of the AACTE, on the National Council for the Accreditation of Teacher Education (NCATE), and other policy bodies; (2) Full membership in AILACTE no longer requires membership in AACTE, a development which will very likely result in more membership for AILACTE and more independence from AACTE; (3) Members of AILACTE's Executive Committee are elected from national geographical regions to insure the fullest national participation; (4) A new publications effort provides expanded opportunities to share perspectives, inform members, and advocate ideas.

A second dimension of the opportunity that confronts liberal arts colleges involves continuing to do what they do best, namely, provide innovative, responsive alternatives to the public domain. Independent governance and small size can be two powerful assets at any time, but when people seek creativity and effectiveness, these qualities are especially useful. The hundreds of independent liberal arts colleges in the United States that are state-approved teacher training institutions provide a pool of diverse models for teachers-in-the-making. Many are empowered by historical and/or religious traditions that embody distinctiveness. Others have taken on educational or ideological foci that would be difficult at best in public systems.

This monograph attempts to shed light on the matter of what these institutions do best by presenting the perspectives of college presidents (and one vice-president) regarding teacher education. Presidents are the spokespersons for their institutions. If teacher education in their midst is to succeed, they must be supporters and constructive critics of it. They must have listening ears to the comments of their colleagues in departments of education and elsewhere in the college who contribute to its impact. They must spread the word about teacher education in liberal arts colleges.

When the idea of a monograph with presidents as contributors was first mentioned at an executive committee meeting of AILACTE, the group was enthusiastic and urged the publications editor to proceed. In the spring of 1989 letters were sent to the presidents of forty-six institutions throughout the United States asking them to contribute. An effort was made to sample colleges that were both large and small, geographically representative of the nation, and that represented various religions and secular ideologies. Most of the invited institutions were members of AILACTE.

The letters included the following statements:

> A new publications effort of AILACTE includes a monograph series. Periodically, we will publish a collection of articles which concentrates on a particular topic. Our first one is tentatively entitled "A View from the Top." It will feature papers by presidents of higher education institutions sharing their views regarding teacher education. We want you to be a contributor to this first volume.

> . . . All contributors are being asked to use the following content guidelines which are purposely brief and straightforward in order to allow you the greatest opportunity to articulate your point of view.

> ADDRESS THE FACTORS THAT IN YOUR JUDGMENT LEAD TO EFFECTIVE TEACHER EDUCATION. In doing so, you may want to single out particular programs of your institution, your education unit, or of other programs that you know. You may want to write about general education, academic majors, and professional education components, respectively. You may want to reflect on aspects of your institution or education unit that are not programmatical or that are not tied to any course. You may want to talk about the size, mission, history, or

student body composition of an institution. In writing about effective teacher education, you may want to dwell on what does not work.

Articles should be between ten and twenty double-spaced typewritten pages in length. Every effort will be made to print them in their entirety as long as they are within these limits.

Sixteen agreed to participate. They come from thirteen states with two from Minnesota and three from Illinois. A number of participants are from colleges with a religious affiliation; the others describe themselves as secular or independent. Enrollment distributions of the colleges are as follows: less than 1000 (Arkansas); 1000 to 1999 (Austin, Beloit, Goshen, Grand Canyon, Hood, North Park, Occidental, Oklahoma Baptist); 2000 to 2999: (Augustana, Concordia, Hope, Luther); over 3000: (Moorhead State, National—Louis University, Teachers College).

A project such as this monograph could not be completed without the help of many people. The Executive Committee of AILACTE has been especially supportive. From the beginning they provided encouragement and insights. At the sixteen campuses of the contributors are secretaries and assistants to the presidents who took care of many behind-the-scenes matters that had to be completed. They deserve a special thank you as does David Heesen, Head of the Beloit College Secretarial Services. David contributed much to the form of the final product.

Thomas Warren
Beloit College
Publications Editor
Association of Independent Liberal Arts Colleges
   for Teacher Education

Introduction

This monograph features college presidents writing about teacher education in liberal arts settings. They reflect on priorities that have been associated with liberal arts colleges for generations, and they share particular ideas and practices that have succeeded or are being introduced at their institutions. They agree that the type of teacher education practiced at liberal arts colleges should be taken very seriously and that the ongoing reformation of American education can learn from it.

One point the presidents make repeatedly is that since liberal arts colleges emphasize teaching excellence throughout the curriculum, teacher education students are regularly in the presence of good teachers during their undergraduate years. This is not to say that good teaching doesn't occur at large public universities, but that the emphasis on teaching is greatest in liberal arts colleges. With this point in mind George Dahlquist of Arkansas Colleges rhetorically asks, "Why should teachers be trained in liberal arts colleges?" His answer: "Because that is where good teaching is recognized, rewarded, nourished and supported." When young teachers who come from liberal arts colleges face unfortunate examples of bad teaching, they will know better. They have seen good teaching in action.

According to the presidents, interchange among the disciplines happens more often on campuses where faculty and students know each other as individuals and are more apt to find ways to work together. It is especially hard for teacher education faculty and students to isolate themselves on a small campus where the theories and methodologies that they teach and learn are refined in the crucible of campus life. Dahlquist, a former teacher, points out that liberal arts colleges encourage students to know their professors outside of the classroom as well as in it. He testifies that "My students babysat my children; I drove 3500 miles roundtrip to New York City with ten students to participate in the National Model United Nations;

1

I performed their marriage ceremonies on campus or in my home . . ."

Interdisciplinariness and openness to fresh ways of recognizing and solving problems are important goals for many liberal arts colleges. By moving easily from one department or division to another within a college, students see interrelationships among ideas. They also recognize similar challenges approached in different ways. George Anderson of Luther College says that Education students who take courses in other departments become accustomed to looking at teaching methods critically. They also receive a lot of feedback on their behavior whether they want it or not. Clearly, the individuality and close working relationships that undergraduates can have with faculty is a powerful attraction and strength of liberal arts colleges.

The emphasis that all teacher training institutions put on individualizing instruction for elementary and secondary pupils receives special reinforcement at colleges where the students themselves are treated as individuals. Martha Church of Hood College opens her article by sharing an anecdote about Nancy Martinez, a teacher in an inner-city neighborhood. Inspired by English and biology teaching that she received in her undergraduate classes, Ms. Martinez is committed to excellence and motivated by a passion for learning similar to those who taught her.

The liberal arts also are enriched by a tie to the practical. Several presidents stress the value that comes from the liberal arts being linked to the world outside of formal education. John Jacobson of Hope College believes that the influence of the practical is not only a benefit to teacher education students, but the whole institution is better off because of it. He says, "The inclusion of education within a liberal arts college is of positive value to the liberal arts. The topics addressed in the preparation of teachers are highly relevant to the liberal arts." President Slaughter of Occidental supports programs that bring together faculty and students from higher education and K–12 public schools. He thinks that the education at both levels improves by working together because education must be a continuum, an integrated whole.

2

Not everyone sees liberal arts colleges as models of teacher education, and President Stoltzfus takes issue with the fact that liberal arts colleges have not been fairly represented in various critiques of American teacher education. "Some of the reports seem to assume that no institution of higher education in the United States is educating prospective teachers effectively . . ." he says. "Much of what the Holmes Group advocates is already happening in the liberal arts colleges." As the leader of a Mennonite institution where working together on campus and in the wider world is a top priority, "One cannot help but smile when we read about educators who have only recently discovered the importance of teaching students to collaborate and co-operate."

In discussing several distinguishing characteristics of liberal arts colleges Paul Dovre of Concordia College (Minnesota) mentions "mission" as first and foremost. The mission of an institution is a unifying force that varies in both intensity and kind among the many liberal arts colleges represented in this volume, but its presence is clear in all of them: contributors speak of morality, excellence, passion for learning, religious heritage, social responsibility, and service.

President Jacobson compares the service-oriented historical goals of liberal arts colleges to those "ornaments of society" whose preoccupation is with accumulation of wealth. The value of a profession is not necessarily commensurate with the price it commands. Jacobson chides those who are not as eager to talk about "my son the teacher" as "my daughter the doctor." A teacher education component in a liberal arts college is a commitment to service according to Jacobson. "Inclusion of pedagogy in the curriculum is a symbol and a reminder that the college is for those who aspire to a life of service as well as for those who aspire to wealth and power. Similarly, in supporting teacher education as part of the liberal arts mission President Anderson asks, "What more honorable path could there be than devoting one's life to the transmission of the best that humanity has learned?

President Agee of Oklahoma Baptist University writes at length about the consensus that has disappeared from American education. He blames an absence of emphasis on values

3

and a diminished development of character as major factors among others.

Orley Herron of National—Louis University provides an historical perspective on change in teacher education. He also suggests that the history of his institution's efforts mirror those of the nation especially at the elementary level. Herron says that the qualitative educational needs of the '90s should get the same attention that was given to the quantitative needs of the period from the end of World War II until 1975.

Several of the colleges represented by presidents in this volume link their religious and ethnic heritage closely to their educational mission. For example North Park College, from its inception affiliated with the Mission Covenant Church, originally based its curriculum on an attempt to prepare Swedish immigrants for involvement in the broader American culture. While the present percentage of first-generation Swedish students is not nearly as large as it used to be, the goal of making an impact on society remains. Teacher education students like all North Park students are expected to be dedicated to Christian witness and service "in the world."

President Stoltzfus emphasizes that Jesus was a role model for great teaching through his use of questions, metaphors, parables, and stories. A community of believers, such as those at a Christian college, can also be considered a community of teachers and learners in which various community members are at different places in their faith development.

President Dovre speaks of the church-related component that adds a unifying value base to the college. President Anderson, whose background has been in theological seminaries as well as undergraduate education, compares effectiveness in the ministry with that of teaching. Both must go beyond their respective subject matter. Roland Dille of Moorhead State University, an English scholar, reflects on literature from his past as he builds a case for what the educated elementary teacher can be. Even though he leads a large public institution, his ideas and values echo those of his counterparts in many small liberal arts colleges.

The point in the preceding examples is that religious and educational goals are woven into an institutional identity which helps to focus values and motivate action. President

Slaughter describes several efforts at Occidental such as "Adopt-a-School" and "math field day" where the teacher education program serves the larger community. Thomas Tredway of Augustana College compares the value-neutral public universities to liberal arts colleges many of which were founded by clergy and other church people. Teachers trained in liberal arts colleges become role models ". . . if not toward the adopting of a particular set of religious ideas or attitudes by the student, then in the encouragement in the young of the thought and reflection that each human must carry on about the development of a personal value system . . ."

Of course service, identity, and motivation are not limited to institutions strongly linked to religion. For example, President Church of independent Hood College describes their scholarship program for promising Black students. Roger Hull of independent Beloit College speaks of the college-initiated "Help Yourself" program which attempts to maximize the opportunity for minority children to ultimately receive a higher education. He also describes a new loan-forgiveness program sponsored by the college and designed to get more liberal arts graduates into the teaching force.

President Timpane of Teachers College notes that the most surprising aspect of the reform movement of the 1980s is that the teacher has been rediscovered. Teachers must be important components in what happens from here on. Timpane shares several promising initiatives involving teachers which have begun during the last five years at his institution. Some of them have implications for all liberal arts colleges that educate teachers.

Several presidents emphasize the crucial role that they should take in supporting teacher education. Harry Smith of Austin College is especially emphatic regarding the role of the president in supporting teacher education. He devotes a substantial part of his article to the form that support can take. Bill Williams of Grand Canyon University is specific in sharing his experience with "participatory management." Martha Church and others discuss forms presidential support directly while some presidents imply as much by virtue of what is done on their home campuses.

5

All college and university presidents must have the cooperation, advice, consent, and enthusiasm of the institution's various constituencies in order to succeed, but in many instances they themselves are the single most important catalysts for change. One of the reasons for choosing presidents to write for this monograph was to put them "on the record" in order to provide guidance for their colleagues who may not be as far along in the support of teacher education.

Liberal Arts Colleges: The Right Crucibles for Teacher Education

John T. Dahlquist
Arkansas College

Whuen asked to write about the role of liberal arts colleges in the training of teachers, I leaped at the chance. I had been a faculty member for sixteen years at two liberal arts colleges before becoming vice president for academic services at yet another liberal arts college where I have been for the last eleven years. I have also served as acting president of that school.

My discipline is history, but I have taught introductory political science courses as well. From the beginning of my career, I have taught students training to be teachers, many of whom have gone on to be fine secondary school and university teachers. Over the years I have talked with many of those students as they matured professionally, and those conversations have helped me better understand how important the liberal arts background is for molding teachers. My thinking was further shaped by a sabbatical experience I had not quite two years ago when I was given the opportunity to .spend two weeks each on four different liberal arts college campuses looking very closely at the way they go about educating students and managing their campuses. Three of those colleges had teacher education programs (all quite different), and talking with their faculty, students and staff helped me see more clearly why liberal arts colleges are the best places to train teachers—for either the K–12 teaching responsibility or college and university teaching.

I have reached the following conclusions after watching countless teachers succeed (and fail) in the "art" of teaching, for I believe it is an art, not a science. I have interviewed dozens of faculty candidates at my college, and after seeing many of those I hired mature as fine teachers, I now know that the liberal arts college is the crucible to refine and train teachers. Why? Because liberal arts colleges give good teaching top priority in recruiting, retaining and rewarding their faculties. Research universities, or even those trying to become large complexes of schools and colleges, reward research and publication over the teaching of students. Even colleges of education in the smaller universities, where research is not demanded on the same level as large universities, require publication for rewards. Students cry out for better teaching, and when they don't see the rewards going to the very best classroom educators, they get the message-education is not about teaching; it is about upward mobility in the education marketplace propelled by publication.

Why should teachers be trained in liberal arts colleges?

First and foremost, because that is where good teaching is recognized and rewarded. It is not my purpose here to define what "good teaching" is. Rather, I wish to argue that it appears most often where it is nourished and supported. This is not to suggest that good teaching can be done without scholarly work, including publication. Good teaching comes from the "overflow" of a lifetime of scholarship. What I want to emphasize is that it is the *teaching* that must be rewarded, not the scholarship.

At my college, as with the others I visited on my sabbatical, one of the protracted debates is over the basis of the faculty reward system. How are faculty to be evaluated in order to determine salary, promotion and tenure? Some variation of our system prevails at the colleges I reviewed. In the annual evaluation at Arkansas College of all faculty—junior and senior, tenured and untenured—about fifty percent of the total weighting of the evaluation is put on the quality of teaching. Peer evaluation and student evaluations determine the final judgment. Twenty percent more of the weighting is put on the

8

counseling and advising roles. The remaining thirty percent is distributed across the other issues of faculty performance: professional disciplinary activity including research and publication, college service, and community service. This balance can be reviewed and revised annually as the faculty member's professional interests and the college's needs vary, but we never move very far away from assigning at least fifty percent of the value of the annual evaluation over to the quality of teaching. Because our salary administration is completely evaluation driven (no COLAs or other across-the-board raises), it is plain to see that one has to be rated consistently as a good teacher to earn long term benefits such as salary increases, promotion and tenure. In addition, we award an endowed prize for "Excellence in Teaching" to further stimulate and reward good teaching.

All of this is by way of arguing that the liberal arts college cares about, and rewards, good teaching. To give the argument even further emphasis, those student teachers of mine whom I talked with about this issue offered the same conclusion. It was the spell of good teaching they fell under and the superlative models they observed that helped them most to become good teachers. All of us can remember some outstanding faculty member we had whom we wish we could imitate in our own lives. I was reminded of that when I received an alumni bulletin featuring a former teacher and mentor of mine who had just died, having celebrated his one hundred-second birthday only a few months before. He had been a Rhodes scholar and an outstanding researcher, who continued to write up to the moment he died. He was an absolutely stunning classroom teacher, both as lecturer and seminar leader. When I think of the splendidly liberating education I received as a teacher-to-be, I know it was from faculty such as he. For those of us who became teachers, models of splendid teaching like he displayed were to lead us all our lives.

Second, liberal arts colleges are where teachers ought to be trained because of their curriculum, and at the heart of that curriculum is a well defined *core*. Let me use our college as an example. We have a prescribed Core Curriculum of 37 hours; every graduate, BA or BS, must take the same Core. It is made up of courses designed to introduce students to skills, vocabularies and thought patterns of the major academic and real-life experiences our faculty believe essential. Every course is carefully designed and monitored. We ask that all the Core courses insinuate writing requirements into their structure. We have just added two new courses to that Core, and both of them have gone through rigorous faculty development and review as they were pilot-tested and revised. My guess is that there will be at least one or two more added to the Core before we have finished shaping it to meet our original "goals and outcomes" statement.

I am not arguing here for our particular Core. I am suggesting, however, that the liberal arts college's notion of a central educational experience rooted in the cultural tradition of the society it serves is one of the basic foods that nourishes good teachers. I, as a teacher, need to know about the most recent hypotheses in cosmological theory, the reason for third world resentment of a threatening U. S. hegemony, or the underlying differences between the romantics' and the existentialists' notion of human nature in order to serve students better. A liberal arts college with a demanding core, that insists every student come to grips with issues as difficult as particle physics or as threatening as social reform, can provide the underlying structure for each student to examine ideas and participate in informed conversation and debate. I believe the opportunity for this to occur is most likely to be at a liberal arts college, and that is why teachers should be trained there.

Third, the liberal arts college requires a "major" of all its degree seekers. This usually is separate from any education requirements that may exist for certification. The three colleges I visited on my sabbatical who were training teachers, had rigorous major requirements, outside the education requirements, for graduates who wished to teach. The concept of every graduate having a substantial and detailed knowledge base in a specific field is very important. The criticism that most often comes my way about secondary school teachers is that they are not "up" on what they are teaching. Not only does the liberal arts major give the student a recent data base, but it also provides the tools and interest in "keeping up" with the newly acquired data. What's more, it is built on the premise that the latter is more important than the former. When a splendid teacher, who is recondite about his/her subject, shows a neophyte that the process of teaching is always backed up by the process of learning, then the model is quite clear. The liberal arts college has the tradition and the commitment to individual disciplines, as well as to a broad-based core, to make the new teacher a well-balanced reservoir of information and ability.

Fourth, the independent liberal arts college is usually flexible enough in its governance system to provide for change when it is necessary. With no state boards of regents, boards of education and legislatures to have to respond to, the liberal arts college can adapt more easily. Even within the private sector of higher education, rapid change is more likely at a liberal arts college than at a similar unit in a private university. As a result, it can offer new programs in its curriculum with a greater alacrity and make it possible to meet students' needs more quickly.

Our college adopted an Honors International Studies Program in 1983 with an emphasis on world politics and global studies which is cross-disciplinary in nature and requires four years to complete. This was done with a minimal expenditure of political energy. Faculty, administration and the board of trustees all had reviewed and accepted the idea within a year of its origin. What's more, that program has drawn students from all over the campus because it is catholic in nature.

Fifth, the liberal arts college is more likely to recognize and reward interdisciplinary study and learning. One of the secondary school teachers I spoke to in preparation for this piece, told me that kind of pedagogy was one of the most important things that had happened to her as she went through college. As a result she learned how to study critical concerns which cut across all segments of society; how problems coming from different sources are resolved; and how scholars with conflicting outlooks can examine an issue from many sides, all helping the student see things more clearly. As a consequence, that clarity of insight leads the student to a new awareness of the multiplexity of the world we live in, thus reducing ethnocentrism and self-smugness. Interchange among the disciplines happens more often on the small campus where faculty know each other and are more apt to find ways of working together.

11

I learned that in my second teaching job, where an art faculty member and I team-taught three different courses. The first was an art/history course we offered in Rome, Italy, and then twice again on our home campus; another was an examination of four important figures of 20th century art; and the third was one on the way humans have viewed their own human form throughout history. Students in those courses, some of whom became teachers, saw two faculty members working together, examining the world through the different eyes of their disciplines, thus bringing complex concepts into a more understandable form. Whether we were successful or not was judged by those students and our peers; but the fact of the matter is, it happened on a liberal arts campus; and it happened there because it is the nature of the liberal arts college to bring together people of different backgrounds and to encourage them to teach together. Large universities have difficulty doing that easily.

Sixth, because liberal arts campuses are small and intimate, they encourage students to come to know their teachers. By doing that, the young teachers-to-be can learn what makes a good teacher tick. They see them at work, struggling to meet deadlines, managing budgets, interacting with other faculty members and arguing ideas. They see how rich and rewarding the life of the teacher is and note that the role of classroom teacher is only a small part of the total person. When the teacher turns mentor, then learning deepens and rewards grow.

One of the exciting things happening on our campus is the growth of faculty/student research projects. So often the young scholar/learner has to wait to get to graduate school for that experience, but not so on a liberal arts campus. Junior and senior undergraduates can participate in meaningful research with their names on finished products. They can join in the sharing of their new found knowledge at regional or national meetings and thus know first-hand the joy of discovery and sharing, which is one of the support systems of good teaching. Undergraduates and faculty working jointly in the learning process are more likely to be found at a liberal arts college. The large university, with its cohorts of graduate students who have to be cared for, may never allow the undergraduate into that process. The liberal arts college can, and does.

In addition, the undergraduate student, in preparing to be a teacher, gets to know the faculty member on a close personal basis because the scale of the liberal arts college allows it. My students babysat my children; I drove 3500 miles roundtrip to New York City with 10 students to participate in the National Model United Nations; I performed their marriage ceremonies on campus or in my home (even one or two in the city park); they came to the math teacher's farm for his annual goat roast; and so the stories go. They learn that a teacher is a fully formed human being, and they come to know that fulfilling the responsibilities of being a teacher requires having a well-developed background, a complete education and emotional maturity. It is an important part of teacher training to allow the student-teacher to gain insight into, and develop a respect for, the broadly developed human being as the quintessential role model for being a teacher. My argument is that this best occurs on the liberal arts campus.

Seventh, students see their faculty on a liberal arts campus in all sorts of settings. The liberal arts college encourages each faculty member to participate in the entire life of the campus. Some faculty don't, but most do, in part because they are interested and in part because they know that such support is vital to the life of the campus. They attend convocations, music programs, athletic events, theatre productions, colloquia and art gallery openings. They are involved in freshmen advisory experiences, extra-curricular activities as advisors, and are supporters of the full life of the campus. Once again, that role model shows the student-teacher that learning takes place on many levels and there is something to be gained by continuing to participate all of one's life.

Finally, teacher education ought to take place on a liberal arts campus where it is one discipline among many. Isolating the training of teachers in schools of education causes too narrow a focus on the professional aspects of educating teachers rather than that of educating students who must continue to be learners all their lives in order to remain good teachers. I have watched with a great deal of interest the way teacher education has flourished when it has to survive in the flower-

13

bed of all the disciplines. I am convinced it is better for college teacher education faculty to be part of the political and ideological struggle of all the disciplines, rather than to remain isolated.

Too often teacher education students have said to me that the courses they took which really helped them were not from the education department, but elsewhere. That sentiment was repeated by more than one student I talked with about this paper. I have watched the teacher education faculty on the two campuses where I have worked over the last twenty-three years, plus those on three of the four campuses I visited on my sabbatical, and everywhere saw the same thing: teacher education programs on liberal arts campuses work very effectively at producing new teachers. Everyday the theories and methodologies taught by the teacher education faculty are refined in the crucible of the entire life of the campus. It is very hard to hide there, and young teachers-in-training are quick to see what is good teaching and what is not, regardless of whatever theories are proffered. It is all around them for the observing. What better place to train teachers?

None of the above is to suggest that teacher education programs on liberal arts campuses are without fault. There are many things that need to be improved all the time. Liberal arts colleges must work to strengthen their teacher education programs in order to attract the very best faculty and make the training of teachers a high budgetary priority. High standards of admission to teacher education programs must be established and met. Education curriculum must be shaped to meet a rising diversity of needs. Supervised teaching during the intern experience must be monitored very carefully. Teachers must not be certified without final and rigorous scrutiny. Success in a teacher education program must never be measured by the completion of credit hours alone. These requirements can be met and maintained by liberal arts colleges because of the high quality to be found in all their disciplines. Teacher education must be treated no differently than all other courses or majors in the continuing self-evaluation process.

Liberal arts colleges can make the difference in teacher training. They can be innovative, responsive, sensitive and daring. They have the ability and creative juices to make the educating of teachers a healthy and happy enterprise. When young teachers who come from liberal arts colleges face unfortunate examples of bad teaching in their daily work place, they will know better. They will have seen good teaching in action. As a result, thousands of them will go on to become role models of splendid teaching in their life's work and will encourage others to do so. It is the heady atmosphere of a vital liberal arts college that brings it all together. Those are the campuses where teachers should be trained.

Teacher Education: Liberal Arts Colleges' Unique Contribution

Thomas Tredway
Augustana College
(Rock Island, Illinois)

Teacher education is of such enormous importance to American culture, that it is a blessing that it is left to no one segment of the higher educational establishment in this land, that it occurs in a variety of contexts, intellectual and institutional. The fact that it continues to be carried on in independent liberal arts colleges is, by my lights, of particular importance. The reasons have to do with the relationship between teacher preparation and the particular characteristics and role of liberal arts colleges in American life.

These institutions are for the most part devoted almost exclusively to undergraduate preparation. The wide range of academic fields and the degrees offered in the large state university are not replicated in these colleges, either on a single campus and not even when all of them—nearly one thousand across the country—are taken collectively. While many offer the Bachelor of Science degree and some professional baccalaureate and masters degrees, their central programs are almost always focused on the Bachelor of Arts curriculum. Many, if not most, of these B.A. programs, are built around two key elements: a considerable number of general education courses in the humanities, fine arts and the social and natural sciences combined with work in a major field of

16

study. These colleges receive students from the wide range of public and private elementary and secondary schools in this country and send them either directly into the professional and business worlds or on to the universities for advanced degrees. They stand, therefore, between the often criticized world of American public education and the greatly envied system of advanced and professional study in the public and private universities of their country. That they graduate a disproportionate (judged by their size) number of future political, business and professional leaders for the nation is clear from data and anecdote alike. Something that occurs in these colleges must be responsible for this fact. It is obvious that this must have to do with their peculiar character, one that makes them unique not just in America but in world-wide higher education.

To begin with, the size of these schools is crucial. Many of these independent liberal arts colleges have only one thousand or fifteen hundred students though a few are as large as three thousand. They emphasize close contact between students and faculty and the direct instruction of beginning students by senior faculty. What their individual academic departments lack in number of faculty and breadth of course offerings is, they claim, made up for by the close working together of students and professors and the effort to have education occur in a familiar and person-centered context. The implications of this for the preparation of teachers is obvious.

Whatever the terrible financial and social constraints that face American public education now and on into the next century, it remains clear that real learning at whatever level or age is often induced by close contact with teachers and mentors, whose attitudes and behavior, as well as whose knowledge and learning, become part of the educational process. Schools and systems which find ways to permit and encourage this kind of contact are fortunate, for it is surely one of the strong signs of a sound educational structure. For teachers to be trained in a college which itself emphasizes this kind of educational experience is perhaps one of the most certain ways to assure that such personalized education will be perpetuated in the public schools where most graduates teach.

These colleges are, as already indicated, liberal arts schools. Their education faculty live, as the institutions themselves do, in the constant and growing tension between the emphasis that their faculties place on breadth of learning (most often expressed through their general graduation requirements) and the insistence of state and other regulatory agencies and associations on increased specialization in professional preparation. Some of these schools, depending on the states for whose educational systems they prepare teachers, have in fact been driven to five-year curricular programs for baccalaureate-level teacher graduates. But this tension between the liberal arts and the professional preparation, however troublesome to deans and department chairs, is one of the hopeful features of teacher training in these colleges, for it suggests that they recognize one essential quality of their work that is often absent elsewhere: the traditional and on-going belief that it is still, in the face of the explosion of knowledge and disciplines, possible to seek some common intellectual and academic core of learning that marks an "educated" woman or man. The good faculty are not all "liberal arts people," but our public educational systems would be undeniably weaker without the leaven that they bring to their careers as teachers.

We have learned in the terrible political crises of this century that persons, even in the highest places, with gilt-edged academic credentials often lacked professional and personal ethical standards of the same lustre. If that were not clear from the tawdry story of the American Watergate crisis, it would be conclusively demonstrated by the role of academics in Hitlerean Germany. In this country the independent liberal arts colleges do not have a corner on virtue and morals. But it is nonetheless true that they share for the most part a unique history, often through their founding by people from a strong religious tradition. Given the separation of church and state in this country and the on-going and applaudable concern that no single religion or ideology control our national life, the public universities remain to a considerable extent value neutral. That is true at least as regards any official espousal of answers to what the intellectual historian Crane Brenton once called the "Big Questions" that life asks every human to

18

consider. Indeed this neutrality is often a matter of pride and satisfaction for staff and leaders in these universities.

That is by and large not the case in the nation's liberal arts colleges, many of which were, as indicated, begun by clergy and church people. That the legal ties between church bodies and colleges have often been severed has not prevented the on-going formal institutionalized recognition through the teaching of religion and the maintenance of chapel programs of the vital and essential place of religion questions (and answers) in academic and personal life. The relationship between religion, culture and the growth of individual values is indisputable. That is not to say that an agnostic humanism is by definition amoral or valueless. It is simply to recognize the fact that in this nation, whether in the theologically profound but non-church going Lincoln or in the morally aggressive and regular Presbyterian Wilson, intellectual and moral leadership has often—indeed usually—been rooted in religious reflection.

The implications for teacher training are clear. No teacher, at least in the public grade and high schools should be allowed (or want) to foist his or her own religious views on pupils. But here again a role model may be more important and effective than an evangelist, if not toward the adopting of a particular set of religious ideas or attitudes by the student, then in the encouragement in the young of the thought and reflection that each human being must carry on about the development of a personal value system and the relationship of these values to ultimate questions about life's origin and destiny. Most simply put, teacher training in the liberal arts college context can make it clear that value neutrality is not necessarily itself a virtue and that for many people in this land value development and religion *are* necessarily connected. It is even possible for a formal religious body to endorse and sustain study and thought about these matters in the college context without seeking to convert every student who enrolls at an institution, as the distinguished records of many church-connected liberal arts colleges demonstrate.

This country's educational system is unique in many ways. Not the least of these is that our people continue to want to support, through taxes, gifts and tuition, a pluralistic system of higher education. People from all over the world want to earn advanced degrees in our graduate and professional schools. The thousands of students who pour into the great state universities, the astounding growth of former "normal schools" into regional universities of quality, the continued leadership in terms of educational quality of our private research universities—all of these attest to the on-going vitality and viability of our university system, even in an age of budget cuts and periodic economic recession. But along with these institutions there continue to exist and flourish the small independent liberal arts colleges, some by the oceans and some on inland rivers. They are sustained, as probably no other segment of American higher education, by the voluntary support of the American people, either through tuition or gifts. That these schools too depend on state scholarships and federal grants is clear. But that our people are willing to go beyond mandated fees and taxes to maintain them is equally clear. Such voluntary maintenance of a pluralistic system of higher education is really unique in the world. If it is to continue, programs of teacher education will play an important role. That is true most of all because of the number of graduates of these colleges who teach and administer in our public and independent elementary and secondary schools. Their training in general education as well as in professional preparation, their own maturing personal and professional values, and their experience of and commitment to the personal as well as the intellectual dimensions of learning are the qualities which make them sought after and appreciated as they develop their careers and those of their pupils and students.

In several ways, then, the independent colleges of the United States are unique. Their focus upon the liberal arts, their concern for value development, their smallness itself—all of these qualities mean that they graduate teachers who are unique. Like the colleges they attended, these people are not *ipso facto* "better." But the very fact of the pluralism that characterizes American education and society means that such people are unique, just as their colleges are. The teachers who graduate from these schools offer a rich source of candidates for elementary and secondary schools, who in their ideas and lives enrich the entire culture through their work.

Presidential Involvement in Teacher Education

Harry E. Smith
Austin College[1]

These are very exciting times in public school education, and those of us who provide leadership for colleges and universities with teacher education programs have a vital responsibility to know what is happening in this field and to support efforts to improve the preparation of future teachers.

Before I describe the ways I feel those "at the top" can improve the education of teachers, it is necessary to describe briefly the teacher education program at Austin College, the institutional context which I know best.

Beginning in 1966, Austin College, a small independent liberal arts college in Sherman, Texas, reworked its traditional four-year teacher education program, having concluded after an extensive self-analysis that quality teacher preparation must combine a broad base of liberal arts learning with practical classroom observation and experience. The philosophy of the Austin Teacher Program (ATP) was stated as follows:

> The Austin Teacher Program has as its primary goal the preparation of teachers, each of whose intellect is informed by the depth and breadth of a vigorous undergraduate education, whose five year development as a classroom teacher is shaped by his or her unique personality, experiential background, and continual growth as a responsible, well-informed, participative, assertive learner, and whose classroom teaching competence is assayed by a cooperative network of education

21

faculty, classroom teachers, and school administrators, all dedicated to the preparation of excellent teachers.

What emerged in 1968 was a five-year master of arts degree program with the following features: a major in an academic discipline—math, English, history, etc.—not education; a series of four credit and noncredit laboratory courses combining theory and practice starting in the freshman year; fifty hours of supervised teaching in the senior year; and a fifth year of thirty-six hours including twelve in the student's academic discipline, twelve in professional courses in such areas as Elementary or Secondary Curriculum Methods, Legal Issues in Education, Research and Synthesis in Education, and Special Education, a four-hour seminar on Instructional Strategies, and an eight-hour practicum or internship involving a full semester of teaching with limited supervision. A research project or thesis is also required for the MA.

Such a program provides ample time for students to explore the teaching profession and to decide whether to continue or opt out based on exposure to real teaching beginning in their freshman or sophomore year in laboratory experiences. It also gives ATP faculty an opportunity to evaluate students and to determine if they should be admitted to the teacher preparation program in their senior year. The program enables students to begin their fifth year with a comprehensive liberal arts education, a completed major, and over 250 hours of classroom experience which begins with observation and ends with actual teaching.

Needless to say, this program has undergone repeated evaluation and change since its initiation. Self-studies in 1972 and 1982 for re-accreditation by the Texas Education Association, a decade review in 1982, and a thorough follow-up study of the 375 graduates between 1972 and 1987 have helped the education faculty determine what revisions have been needed to prepare students more adequately for classroom teaching. There have also been annual alumni follow-up surveys to assess the effectiveness of the program in the light of actual teaching experience. Annual "Bright Ideas" conferences have brought alumni back to campus to describe their teaching experiences for ATP faculty and students, and a newsletter has helped graduates keep in touch and benefit from each other's experiences.

Significant modifications have included letting ATP faculty serve as primary supervisors for undergraduate classroom experiences; relying more on local teachers as supervisors at the graduate level; providing more thorough preparation for internships; increasing the number of fifth year internships in place of closely supervised student teaching; developing a team approach in most courses; increasing the emphasis on computer-based instruction; and offering students opportunities to serve as tutors in Grayson County's Cooperative Early Education Program for At-Risk Students.

Serious study is currently being given by the ATP faculty to reworking the program's basic goals; revising or abolishing the introductory, partial-credit laboratory course; increasing academic credit for the sophomore and junior year laboratory courses; expanding the research component; incorporating more content pedagogy; and exploring ways to stay abreast of developments in educational technology. Attention is also being given to distinguishing more clearly the content and requirements of graduate and undergraduate courses in the liberal arts disciplines, a necessary task in an institution where teacher education is the only graduate program.

Although this unique five-year program was already in place when I came to Austin College in 1978—and I had no part in its design—I have been an enthusiastic supporter of the Austin Teacher Program and have considered it a distinctive part of our institutional mission. It has certainly enhanced the College's reputation, earning two national awards from the American Association of Colleges for Teacher Education and recognition from the Carnegie Commission for the Improvement of Teaching.

I believe that presidential support for teacher education programs should take several forms:

1. *Ensuring that adequate resources are available for the program.* At a time when financial resources are seldom adequate to cover institutional needs, presidential leadership involves making hard choices about the allocation of limited resources (something I am acutely aware of as we work each year to arrive at a balanced budget), and providing adequate

funds for faculty and programs. It also involves resisting the tendency in liberal arts institutions to reduce the budget of professional programs and recognizing that teacher preparation programs are labor intensive and seldom cost efficient. Presidential leadership also necessitates ensuring that faculty recruited for such programs have the kind of credentials, skills, and experiences which will bring credit to the program and command the respect of faculty in other disciplines. In short, it means making sure that the program, facilities, and staffing all reflect a strong administrative commitment to maintaining a quality teacher education program.

I was reminded recently about the need for this type of support as we recruited for an education faculty position and were made acutely aware of the inadequacy of the facilities which house our teacher preparation program. Although the ATP is located in a separate building (formerly known as the College's powerhouse) that has many interesting spaces for displays of teaching resources, computer hardware, course planning, and faculty-student interaction, the building itself needs to be refurbished or replaced. Providing needed facilities is an important way that leadership at the top can make clear to students and faculty a college's commitment to its teacher education.

In short, I know of no institution with a strong teacher education program which does not have the enthusiastic support of the president and an administration willing to see that the program is adequately funded, housed, and staffed.

2. *Encouraging education faculty to develop a clear vision of the role of teacher education in the institution, community and region and then supporting that vision.* At a time when education programs are receiving scathing criticism and their credibility is in serious question, it seems especially important to insist that those who train teachers have a clear sense of their relationship to the total educational enterprise, the competencies they seek to develop, the values they hope to instill, and the assumptions behind their curriculum, as well as their willingness to engage in nondefensive discussion with others about their program. Education faculty in liberal arts colleges must also have a clear vision of the unique roles their programs play in relation to larger, public teacher education programs.

They must have a strong sense of how their programs complement programs in the public sector as well as how they are distinctive. And they must make their programs' unique roles known to prospective students, the general public, and legislators. Presidents and their information and admission officers can take a proactive lead in presenting their teacher education programs to these various constituencies.

On their own campuses presidents can play an important part not only in defending the importance of strong teacher preparation programs for their institutions, countering efforts to diminish these programs in relation to traditional disciplines or pre-med, pre-law, and business majors, but also in helping to dispel some of the prevailing misconceptions about education faculty, courses, and students. At the same time, presidents must insist that quality standards be maintained and must support the efforts of education faculty to be more selective in screening and retaining students in their programs. It also means recognizing that few traditional instruments for course evaluation can adequately assess the kind of one-on-one teaching and learning which teacher education programs utilize. Teaching through classroom observation and supervision, and directing research projects and theses, in addition to traditional classroom lectures and seminar discussions, require different ways for assessing performance, contact hours, and productivity. A president's supporting role also requires acknowledging that the experiential nature of teacher education requires special career development options; periodic return to classroom teaching or administration in an elementary, secondary, or high school; strong support structures for faculty; and frequent participation in professional workshops.

3. *Initiating communication and developing trust with local school officials.* A program which emphasize observation and participation in actual classroom teaching requires collaborative relationships with the administrators and teachers of area schools. It is crucial that school officials understand the program, respect the faculty, and regard the college's teacher program as a resource for rather than a burden on the local school system.

25

This may mean negotiating released time for which the college pays local teachers to serve as mentors or supervisors, hiring school administrators and teachers to serve as adjunct faculty, or making the college's learning resource center available to area teachers. It may also involve sponsoring workshops on new teaching methods or recent research on teaching or offering special courses for teacher certification and continuing education on classroom management, different styles of teaching and learning, or the applications of computer assisted instruction.

A standing committee composed of representatives from Austin College and the Sherman Independent School District meets regularly to enhance the college-school relationship, giving special attention now to cooperative efforts in implementing provisions of the career ladder outlined by Texas' new education law. It also means having one of our professors direct the Texoma Cooperative Teacher Education Center through which the College and twelve districts in the north Texas area address issues related to the education of teachers. For the past two years, Austin College has attracted hundreds of young people and their teachers to campus for a "Celebration of Imagination," a writing festival and teacher workshop, led by such writers and artists as Byrd Baylor, Elizabeth Ellis, Mary Kitagawa, and Orin Cochrane.

Building positive relationships with teachers and administrators should also involve faculty from other departments. At Austin College the Foreign Language Department sponsors an annual Foreign Language Weekend, which this past spring brought over one thousand French, Spanish, German and Latin high school language students and their teachers to campus for competitions and cultural activities. During the past three years the college's Latin faculty have conducted a summer institute for groups of twelve to fourteen high school classics teachers. The purpose of the institute is to explore ways to make the teaching and learning of Latin more exciting in Texas high schools.

4. *Keeping up with development in teacher education and encouraging innovation and change.* With all that presidents have to read in order to keep up with changes in federal funding, tax law, liability insurance, curriculum reform, as-

sessment, and governance revisions, it is impossible to read all of the many studies on the weaknesses and needs of teacher education programs which are available today. Nevertheless, presidents must try to understand the implications of recent education reforms, proposed changes in certification standards, and the ways other institutions are responding to the need to restructure their programs.

I have been fortunate to have a good relationship with the faculty of the Austin Teacher Program, and to have their help in keeping up with recent developments in teacher education, as they pass on to me materials from the state, regional, and national conferences they attend as an integral part of their job. I have been impressed with their ongoing discussions, collaboration, and openness to change, as well as their keen desire for a program whose graduates know how to use teaching strategies creatively and effectively with different types of students and classroom environments, who can interact easily with their students, and who can tolerate onerous institutional demands. The ATP faculty also endeavor to help their students become teachers who can reflect critically on what is happening in their classrooms, schools, and communities and who know that their education as teachers is a never-ending process which requires a commitment to professional and personal growth throughout a career and lifetime.

My respect for the Austin Teacher Program has been heightened by my own teaching experience in the program. In a January Term course on "Teaching and Learning with Simulation Games," I was impressed with the flexibility and creativity of the students from the teacher education program. They seemed especially appreciative of the instant feedback which simulation games provide, the importance of role playing, and the value of autotelic learning.

In a Contemporary Policy Students course on "What's Right and Wrong with our Schools and Colleges?" which I co-taught with a member of the ATP faculty, I noted the openness of education students to collaborative learning in which they worked in small groups to research and propose specific policies and strategies for dealing with such issues as classroom discipline; curricula for small, rural schools; gender perspectives in educational goals and assessment; non-traditional,

27

experiential learning; cultural illiteracy, and development of critical thinking.

My appreciation for teacher education programs has also been enhanced by having a daughter who graduated from the Austin Teacher Program. Now in her third year as an elementary teacher in the Houston area, she has demonstrated many of the skills and competencies which the Austin Teacher Program seeks to develop in its students, and she continues to be excited about the opportunities she is having to apply what she learned at Austin College.

5. *Expecting teacher education programs to demonstrate their effectiveness.* Within the past decade educators have witnessed a crescendo of calls for reform. Governors, state legislators, federal education officials, newspaper editors, and the general public have demanded greater accountability and assurances of quality from elementary and secondary schools and higher education. Reports such as *A Nation at Risk* and *Quality—Higher Education's Principal Challenge* have underscored the challenges which this nation faces in promoting quality education at all levels. Since teacher preparation programs constitute a primary link between colleges and schools, it is especially incumbent upon education faculty to articulate or clarify the goals of their programs and to develop ways of assessing and demonstrating student achievement. I believe that assessment that is consonant with the mission of an institution and the goals of a teacher preparation program can improve teaching, encourage collaboration, and provide a catalyst for program renewal.

Presidents have an obligation to ensure that faculty will have the resources to develop and implement assessment strategies. They must see that faculty have ample opportunity for training in assessment and evaluation methods, including both qualitative and quantitative techniques. And they must support these efforts even in the face of resistance from other quarters in the institution.

6. *Lobbying on legislative or regulatory policies which affect teacher education.* College presidents have a special responsibility today to monitor the legislation which many state legislatures and accrediting bodies are enacting which significantly impact the content and staffing of teacher prepara-

tion programs. In several states, for example, bills are being considered which would limit certification of teachers to those who graduate from public institutions, prompting the presidents of colleges related to one Protestant denomination to organize in opposition to such legislation. In other states, efforts have been made to require accreditation by the National Council for Accreditation of Teacher Education as a condition for certifying the graduates of teacher education programs.

Members of Independent Colleges and Universities of Texas (ICUT) have worked with the organization's lobbyist in Austin to ensure that changes in the state's accreditation requirements do not discriminate against private institutions. This has required vigilance on the part of the independent college presidents and a willingness to visit, write, and call legislators to lobby for standards that do not pose insurmountable obstacles for the reaccreditation of teacher education programs at small, independent colleges. Here again I have found myself in frequent contact with our education faculty to be sure that I understand all the nuances of proposed legislation and to share with them the information I receive about proposed changes which could seriously affect the future of our program.

College presidents cannot (and should not) take on their already overburdened shoulders the responsibility for running their institution's teacher education program; they have provosts and deans and department chairs to do that. Yet I am convinced that presidents can and do play a decisive role in shaping the teacher education programs on their campuses. I am also convinced that college administrators "at the top" can do far more than they have done in the past to ensure that their teacher preparation programs are graduating students who are able to cope creatively with the increasingly difficult job of being effective classroom teachers.

Note

1. I am indebted to Todd Hutton, Assistant to the President and Assistant Professor of Education at Austin College, for collaboration in the writing of this chapter. H.E.S.

Dollars and Sense in Educating Teachers

Roger H. Hull, President
Beloit College[1]

Not everyone believes in the liberal arts—unfortunately. Although it is hard for me, as the president of a liberal arts college, to understand how anyone could question the value of a liberal arts education, some individuals do. Perhaps it is parental pressure to prepare for particular positions; perhaps it is self-imposed pressure by students "to do something useful." Whatever the reason, though, those who fail to get a liberal arts education are in my view less effective (and less enlightened) than their liberal arts counterparts.

Teacher education presents an obvious case in point. Even though the administrator in me says that we should do what we can in the four years that we have students on our campus and that we should then turn them loose to do what they can, the idealist in me has a different perspective. Students should—students must if they are to be effective teachers—get an exposure to a wide range of liberal arts and science courses and an opportunity to go into some depth in a particular field. Without an understanding of the relationships between and among different branches of learning, students cannot become effective teachers. It simply is not enough for a student to learn something about her or his field and develop different techniques and skills to convey that knowledge to students. It simply is not enough!

Ideally, a student should first develop breadth and depth. Then he or she can develop the requisite approaches to conveying the knowledge that has been obtained through study. However, if we continue to insist that students focus on teacher education, without first developing that breadth and depth, we are failing both that student and the students who will in turn be "taught" by that student/teacher. In short, I believe that there is a direct relationship between a student's liberal arts education and her or his effectiveness in a classroom in subsequent years and that the less a student learns the less effective a teacher that student will become.

Traditionally, the goal has been to cram teacher education coursework and other coursework into four years. At larger universities which may not have broad-based requirements outside of the major, students simply lack the required breadth (and probably depth). Yet, even at liberal arts colleges, at least those in states with onerous (in terms of numbers of courses) teacher certification requirements, the cramming of teacher education coursework into four years dilutes what might otherwise be a first-rate education. The result: Future teachers fulfill teacher education requirements, but, in the process, they paradoxically become less effective teachers.

Although many students graduate from a college or university and choose to enter the teaching profession, too few of them do so, and those that do all too often forfeit a part of their education which would make them better teachers. In the long run, neither they nor society is benefitted because, as dedicated as they might be, they simply have to be less prepared than would be the case if all of their undergraduate studies were dedicated to the liberal arts and sciences.

At Beloit College we have decided to address this issue in a meaningful way. We want to invest in better teachers, not in more rhetoric.

What we are prepared to do is to offer a "free" fifth year to students who want a full undergraduate liberal arts education at the College and who would like to be teacher certified. The fifth year tuition will be "loaned" to those students, with the stipulation that 25% of the tuition costs will be cancelled for each year that the student teaches at the elementary or secondary school level. In effect, therefore, the fifth year is free to students after they have taught for four years in K through 12 schools.

Depending on the results of the program, we might expand it to include non-Beloit College students who have completed undergraduate studies in the liberal arts. As a prerequisite for such an extension, we have discussed restricting the program to those with strengths in areas in which the United States is weak or in which the Beloit community has a specific problem to address. For instance, we might provide the cancellable fifth year loans for liberal arts graduates from other institutions who have majored in either languages or the sciences, or we might provide a fifth year to Black or Hispanic liberal arts graduates from other schools who agree to teach in Beloit public schools.

By following the cancellable loan model, we at Beloit want to encourage students to pursue careers in teaching which they might otherwise forego for financial reasons and to make those future teachers more effective. Some might argue (rightly) that this investment by a college might not make great financial sense. It may not on the "bottom line," but it arguably can attract idealistic students with an interest in teaching, and, in truth, the real costs are fairly limited. Yet no one can argue with the merits of the proposition.

The commitment of Beloit College to teacher education is also demonstrated at another level. If it is important for a college to try to find ways to educate its students both within and outside the classroom (and it is), then it is equally important for the college to focus on the most effective means to provide that education. One clear example of what we do is to be found in the teacher training experiences that students have been involved with in elementary and secondary schools in Britain (and that we are exploring in Latin America and Japan)—and that students may sacrifice if they cram coursework and teacher certification into four years.

However, a more dramatic example exists on the Beloit College campus itself. In February 1988, Beloit College announced a program for minority youth in the greater Beloit area. Called "Help Yourself," the program is a three-pronged effort to have an impact on the education of minority youth (Blacks, Hispanics, Asian Americans, and Native Americans) in Beloit.

32

The first stage of the program, the Beloit Academy, began in the fall of 1988 and entailed the selection of 24 fourth-grade students from among the 44 students who applied. The students come to campus after school three days a week for one hour, three hours on Saturday, and four weeks in the summer for a *Latin*-based curriculum. Why Latin? Because it was determined by the faculty to whom we turned for guidance in this area that Latin was the best way for students to develop their analytical skills.

The faculty is ours; the program is conducted on the college campus; the cost is ours. Yet, it is important to note that we are working with the Beloit Public School System, for we concluded that we wanted their support if we were to make an investment of this magnitude. Fortunately for all, Beloit school officials view the program as the positive force that we believe it is.

As a focal point for the class, the city of Alexandria, Egypt, was chosen. The selection of Alexandria, in the time frame of the second century A.D., gives the students an opportunity to learn about history, geography, philosophy, mathematics, and physics. To see fourth graders with an understanding of these concepts is, in this day and age, highly unusual. The manner in which they learn these subjects is even more unusual, for how often does one read about fourth graders, especially disadvantaged youth, learning about beached boats in Africa which they then learn to move by practicing with a fulcrum on a dumpster? How great the excitement as the fourth graders learn this principle of physics! How great the excitement for the faculty to see the expressions on the faces of those 24 youths!

We will stay with these 24 fourth graders, if they will stay with us, through elementary and secondary school. Although each student has already dramatically improved in school, we feel that our investment in them has only begun. It is an investment that we are happy to make, and we will continue to make it so long as the students and their family (or their parental surrogates) also make an investment. What is their investment? It is that each student has to agree to be a mentor for students following in the next year, and the parent, or surrogate has to agree to come to the Saturday sessions because we want them to recognize the importance of the process (and because they must feel that there is a *quid pro quo* for the College's investment in them).

After "graduation" from the Beloit Academy at the end of eighth grade, students will enter the Pre-Collegiate Program, the College's program for grades nine through twelve, and come to Beloit for four weeks in the summer. We will continue our investment in them by working with them until they graduate from high school, by striving to develop their skills across the curriculum, and by giving them the opportunity to take Beloit College classes.

Following their graduation from high school, the students will have the opportunity to continue their studies wherever they wish—and we believe those students will, as a result of their education for the previous nine years, be in great demand. We have also committed to take at Beloit College up to five students a year and to meet the full financial needs of those students during their undergraduate years. The latter commitment has already begun because we have taken area high school students in the Pre-Collegiate Program, worked with them for three years, and, after their graduation from high school, admitted them to the College (we had three last year and will have five this year).

"Help Yourself" is important to a wide range of constituencies. It is obviously important to the students in the program because their lives will be transformed; it is important to the minority community because future leaders will be developed; it is important to Beloit College because this college—and all colleges—must prepare for a changing student body; and it is important to the students at the College because it provides a wonderful opportunity for a combination of volunteerism and practical experience.

On this last point, the opportunity presented for teacher education students to "practice teach" with these fourth and fifth and sixth and seventh and eighth graders is outstanding. Not only will their involvement in "Help Yourself" give students a sense of satisfaction, but it will also better prepare them for their chosen career. In this sense, "Help Yourself" helps all.

Teacher education in the liberal arts setting provides many opportunities for prospective teachers. To the extent that liberal arts colleges are also willing to do some innovative work financially for those teachers and for students in elementary and secondary schools, the opportunity for teacher education is clearly enhanced.

Although the jury will be out for some time as to whether more students will be encouraged into the teaching ranks through our financial incentive or whether students engaged in "Help Yourself" will prosper, I have no doubt on either score. Our programs will benefit both teachers and students—and, in the process, they will benefit Beloit College, too.

Liberal arts learning is all about exploring new frontiers. We feel that these two efforts have given us a good foothold on the teacher education frontier.

Note

1. Roger Hull is now the President of Union College and the Chancellor of Union University (Schenectady, New York).

Restoring the Balance

Paul J. Dovre
Concordia College
Moorhead, Minnesota

For most of the decade of the 80's, educational reform has been at the center of college and university agenda. Independent commissions, federally sponsored studies, and educational associations have contributed to the agenda. All of this has been occasioned by the perception that education is not meeting national goals and that the quality and quantity of teachers is declining. For all of these reasons, we are, in the words of the formative study document of the decade, "a nation at risk."

Among the institutions standing at the nexus between societal needs and academic excellence is the independent liberal arts college. Because of its small size, its holistic program and its historic reputation for quality, the independent college is a special resource for educational reform. On the other hand, the reform movement and the accreditation community have been dominated by large and public institutions with graduate school perspectives on what is principally an undergraduate issue. As a consequence, some of the so-called reform measures proposed by national commissions and accrediting agencies could endanger the teacher preparation programs of independent colleges. For that reason, we must restore the balance between qualities indigenous to teacher education institutions and those standards promulgated by external agencies and groups. This brief paper will make the case for the integrity of teacher preparation programs in

36

independent liberal arts colleges and suggest ways in which they can be preserved and provide a model for the reform of teacher education.

Teacher education programs at independent liberal arts colleges are distinguished by characteristics of missions, coherence, community and creativity.

MISSION: Independent colleges have a unifying conception of education centered in the liberal arts and integration into that vision is one of the characteristics of teacher education programs in those institutions.[1] While each institution expresses this vision in unique ways, the unifying characteristics include exposure to the liberating arts and sciences, a strong base in the humanities, a common core of academic experiences and the development of problem-solving and communication skills. Special emphasis is usually placed on the ways of knowing unique to each discipline as well as the interdependence of the disciplines. Independent colleges require a greater percentage of coursework in the liberal arts' core subjects than do public institutions.[2]

Clarity about mission is a central agenda at Concordia. Faculty take great care in articulating mission and understanding its implications for their work. The benefits of this clarity about mission are several. First, students see their education in a more holistic way and experience the interdependence of skills and knowledge. Second, criteria for faculty recruitment and programs for faculty development can be directed toward institutional mission. Third, enrolling students tend to better understand the expectations for their academic performance. Fourth, faculty expectations are more clearly identified: They are expected to contribute to the liberal arts' mission by teaching their courses in a liberating way and teaching ability is preeminent among the criteria for professional advancement. Fifth, clarity about the liberal arts' mission is also helpful in program development and curriculum assessment. At Concordia a college-wide curriculum committee monitors all curriculum proposals in terms of common criteria. Courses that compose the liberal arts core are assessed regularly in terms of college-wide expectations.

The liberal arts tradition has strong support from professionals, business leaders and teacher educators. In a recent address, Lee S. Shulman from the Stanford University School of Education made a strong endorsement of the liberal arts when he said, "undergraduate arts and science education is, in its own way, one of the most successful examples of teacher education I have ever documented."[3] For the typical liberal arts college, the liberal arts are the focus for all programs of study including teacher education. This clarity of mission is, I submit, a unique resource to teacher preparation programs in independent colleges.

The second characteristic of liberal arts programs at independent colleges is COHERENCE. As noted above, students and faculty work at discovering and experiencing the interdependence of disciplines. No academic program is sufficient unto itself. In particular, education programs are built with an awareness of the knowledge and skills contributed by the several disciplines to which students are exposed. This leads to an integration of liberal arts and teacher preparation programs that is mutually enriching. For example, at Concordia several essential kinds of awareness and skills are denoted as cross-curricular matters including global awareness, verbal competence, computer literacy and inclusive education. Each emphasis is essential to teacher preparation and competence is the responsibility of every discipline rather than a single academic department. Several members of the education department teach courses in the core curriculum while others have offered workshops to the whole faculty on research in teaching. The coherence of the academic program is also underscored by the fact that curriculum development in teacher education is the product of interdepartmental planning.

COMMUNITY is the third distinguishing characteristic of independent liberal arts colleges. Most of our colleges are small in size and that fact lends itself to collegiality and common spirit. Decision-making involves people from every campus constituency and addresses nearly every aspect of campus life including curriculum development; personnel decisions; budget, faculty and facility planning, and student life programs. By way of illustration, in Concordia's most recent long-range planning effort, members of the Education Department played key roles. The departments involved in teacher preparation are key players in the governance of the teacher education

38

program through the Teacher Education Committee. And when regular peer evaluations of faculty are conducted, participation of faculty from other department is mandatory. In all of these ways, teacher education is in the mainstream of the College's life.

Most independent colleges are church-related which adds a unifying value-base to the dimensions of community one experiences on the campus. There is a strong element of mutual concern in communities of our size and such values are frequently articulated and tested in the common life. In their study of independent colleges, Rule and Stanton of St. Louis University found that these institutions were able to meet value goals because of "the integrated environment of their campuses."[4] Indeed, over the years church-related colleges have developed expertise in addressing value issues in a way which is both thoughtful and nonparochial.

Faculty-staff mentoring is another element common to the independent liberal arts community. While the concept is not unique to these campuses, the size and mission of independent colleges enables them to treat this function with particular focus. Again, the work of Rule and Stanton identifies the special strengths of student/faculty relationships at small liberal arts colleges.[5] At Concordia we have described the teacher as a role model of inquiry, the liberal arts and the Christian life. In a faculty document these roles are described and expectations are defined. For example, faculty members are to be models of inquiry in the ways they approach their continuing education, research and teaching. Faculty at Concordia relate to students, both academically and personally, in ways that the reform reports would like K–12 teachers to relate to their students. Since we know that teachers will teach as they have been taught, this role modeling of faculty at independent colleges is a very powerful influence on future teachers. Again, the size and mission of the independent institution facilitates a high degree of focus and consensus on such goals and values.

Another value that is natural to independent colleges is academic excellence. This is true in part because most of our students have high ability and are achievement-oriented. Traditions of outstanding achievement by graduates also underscore the commitment to excellence. This value tends to permeate the community and motivate both faculty and students in their respective vocations.

CREATIVITY is another distinguishing characteristic of teacher education programs at independent liberal arts colleges. The education tradition in America has always prized diversity, and independent colleges have been singled out as sources of program innovation. Perhaps owing to size and flexibility as well as tradition, independent colleges have been prolific in developing program models for all of higher education.

At Concordia the Education Department developed an innovative model for the preparation of elementary teachers more than a decade ago. The elementary education program includes a pre-student teaching semester in which students participate in clinical experiences in local schools for half-days for ten weeks. As students are introduced to teaching methodology on campus, they can practice what they learn with children in active school settings. College faculty and classroom teachers provide opportunities for discussion, reflection and growth in teaching skills. This clinical model is very similar to the clinical models suggested by some reform reports for post-graduate teacher education programs.

Another innovation was the development of an experiential program for learning about the language and culture of other nations in village settings. Initiated by a professor in the Education Department, this total immersion concept of learning now reaches over 7,000 young people each year in a total of ten languages. Teacher preparation has been part of this program for 20 years and a foundation-supported program now provides experienced teachers with an opportunity to integrate aspects of this experiential learning model into traditional classroom settings.

Recently the secondary education program at Concordia was redesigned to include a greater emphasis on the structure of knowledge in various disciplines, the use of technology in education, and research on teaching. Courses and clinical experiences in the local schools are designed to create student cohort groups and develop interdependence among students, college faculty, and classroom teachers. And as a final example of innovative service, one year ago Concordia became a partner of the Valley and Lakes Educational District in which local rural school districts and post-secondary institutions have joined efforts to enhance the quality of educational service for learners of all ages. Two recent cooperative projects are an interactive telecommunications system linking all participants and a curriculum assessment and improvement program for selected K–12 programs.

In sum, teacher education programs at independent liberal arts colleges are a special resource owing to the distinguishing characteristics of these institutions. While the unique integrity of these programs should be both recognized and encouraged, the trend of recent reform and certification efforts both ignores and undermines this uniqueness. While one can hardly quarrel with the intention and analysis of most education reform efforts, we must take time to weigh their consequences. As Wimpelberg, King and Nystrom[6] noted, most reforms ignore differences among colleges and, in particular, often ignore the implications for education programs based in private liberal arts colleges.

One can specify this analysis in a number of ways. To begin with, one might note the probing analysis of the Holmes group which identified a number of qualitative issues and goals. The irony is that at the heart of their recommendations was a quantitative solution which essentially defines a new and tighter professional straightjacket for teacher education programs. In our own college in recent years, we have experienced a spate of new requirements which ignore the individuality of our program, undermine our flexibility and jeopardize the liberal arts experience of our students. For example, the faculty load for teacher supervision has been decreased by 50 percent, the length of the student teaching experience has been expanded by 25 percent, courses have been added to the art and biology education programs, pre-school teaching experiences in the schools have been expanded, and public school teachers have been added to curriculum and policy committees. All of these changes were mandated by either state or national accrediting bodies. Some of the changes may be helpful and others were already in process. But my concern is that these mandates do not discriminate on the basis of institutional size or type, the design of individual programs, the institu-

41

tional context or the characteristics of the total academic program. Faculty senate and curriculum committee members on our campus are increasingly frustrated about how we shall be able to retain the integrity of our educational mission as a liberal arts college and, at the same time, maintain our teacher preparation program. Another hidden consequence of these so-called reforms is the substantial load of reporting and bureaucratic tape unwinding that is thrust upon those educators who serve as deans and department chairs.

A decade ago accrediting groups said that institutions could design their own teacher education programs and that they would look only at the outcome, the product of the program. But this view really never came into fashion as goals began to be translated into courses, skills into curricula, and expectations into credit hours. Public institutions with schools and colleges of education may be able to navigate such intrusions but independent liberal arts colleges are jeopardized by them. Given the richness of our tradition in teacher education and the quality of our students, graduates and faculty, this is a trend which could put both the educational establishment and society "at risk" in yet another way.

All of this is not to suggest that the education reform movement be dismissed for it has focused national attention on critical issues and in many cases accrediting agencies have assisted institutions in strengthening their programs. But the analysis I have outlined does call for restoring the balance between external agency demands and internal program integrity.

Independent liberal arts colleges will need to take some initiatives. For starters, independent colleges should re-examine their commitment to teacher education programs. Teacher preparation cannot be done half-way, half-heartedly or as a mere "convenience" to students. Teacher education must be an integral part of, and an asset to, a college's mission or it should be eliminated. Programs that are tangential to mission or inadequately supported shortchange their students and undermine the reputation of teacher education at all independent colleges. Next, we must spread the word about the uniqueness of education programs in our sittings. "Think globally and act locally" is the theme of the Internationalists which can be applied equally well to the current education crises. "Think nationally and act locally" is, in effect, the theme of much current reform in public education where local faculties, school boards, and communities are being encouraged to devise reform strategies which best utilize their resources and, at the same time, meet local and national needs. Such a strategy fits the genius of the independent liberal arts college and we would do well to adopt this reform strategy in dialogues with accrediting agencies and reform commissions. It is a strategy which requires flexibility in the application of standards to institutions and encourages diversity in approaches to teacher preparation.

Notes

1. Whimelberg, Robert K., Jean A. King, and Nancy J. Nystrom. (n.d.) Private Teacher Education: Profiles and Prospects. In Alan R. Tom, (ed.), *Teacher Education in the Liberal Arts Settings*. American Association of Colleges for Teacher Education and the Association of Independent Liberal Arts Colleges for Teacher Education, 23.

2. Rule, Ann M. and Charles M. Stanton, (n.d.) Private Teacher Education: Profiles and Prospects. In Alan R. Tom, (ed.), *Teacher Education in the Liberal Arts Settings*. American Association of Colleges for Teacher Education and the Association of Independent Liberal Arts Colleges for Teacher Education, 14.

3. Shulman, Lee S. (1989) Toward a Pedagogy of Substance. *AAHE Bulletin* 41, no.1O (1989): 11.

4. Rule, op. cit., p. 16.

5. Rule, op. cit., p. 17.

6. Whimelberg,op. cit., p. 22.

Small is Beautiful: Teacher Education in the Liberal-Arts Setting

Victor E. Stoltzfus[1]
Goshen College

As a liberal-arts college affiliated with the Mennonite Church, Goshen College provides a setting especially congenial to undergraduates who wish to prepare themselves for the profession of teaching. First, as a Christian college, Goshen grounds itself in the history and tradition of a religion whose central figure was a great teacher. Any student seeking an excellent example of the Socratic method need only read one of the four gospels. Again and again, Jesus answered questions with questions. He was a spellbinding storyteller who used parables and metaphors to convey his message.

It might be said that, in Christianity, teaching has always been viewed as the primary means for accomplishing the primary goal; one concordance of the Bible lists 268 Old and New Testament passages in which the words *teach, teacher, teachers, teaches, teaching* and *teachings* are used. In Christ's "Great Commission" to his disciples, he instructed them to "go and make disciples of all nations ... teaching them to obey everything I have commanded you" (emphasis added).[2]

The "Great Commission" shows how vital teaching is to the Christian faith. Jesus did not exhort his disciples to win converts through military conquest, political activity or economic dominance; they are to be won through teaching using both conventional teaching techniques and the power of personal example.

Second, Goshen College tries to incorporate Mennonite beliefs into the teacher-education program. Unlike some other faiths and denominations in the United States, the Mennonite Church does not embrace our nation's competitive, individualistic, compartmentalized ethos. Mennonites cannot help but smile when we read about educators who have only recently discovered the importance of teaching students to collaborate and cooperate, who now view parents as partners in learning rather than nuisances, and who now recognize the importance of integrating different subjects into schoolwork, rather than isolating those areas into narrowly defined subject areas.

Mennonites have long known the truth articulated well by John Muir, the great naturalist: "Whenever we try to pick out anything by itself, we find it connected to everything else in the universe." We strive to integrate our religious faith into every aspect of our lives. Of course, Mennonites attend church, but we also believe that our standards of living, our behavior in interpersonal relationships and our behavior at work or in the classroom should reflect our beliefs.

We believe we are called to live, work and worship in a community of believers, supporting one another emotionally, spiritually and materially when the need arises. Because we all are at different points in our faith development, the community of believers could also be called a community of teachers and learners, in which each person is both a teacher and a learner. Coming from this background gives our teacher-education students an advantage. Although many of our students come from Mennonite and related backgrounds, before coming to GC they may not have experienced a community where religion, education and everyday life were integrated to such a degree. We hope their GC experience will help them appreciate the community of believers and enable them to create a community of teachers and learners in their classrooms.

The third factor which enhances the teacher-education program at Goshen College is that GC is a liberal-arts college. Because Mennonites embrace the idea of community and collaboration, the ideal of a community of scholars and the pur-

 GOSHEN COLLEGE LIBRARY
GOSHEN, INDIANA

pose of such a community — to teach students how to learn, instead of teaching them mere facts — is not foreign to Mennonites. Indeed, the liberal-arts model of higher education fits better with our beliefs than others. As we prepare students to respond to God's call, we know that that call very likely may not lead them to professions with carefully delineated "career ladders" culminating in a corner office on the top floor, but instead to an inner-city school, a remote African outpost or a tiny town in Appalachia.

Goshen College's motto, "Culture for Service," also reflects our view of the liberal arts. GC does not view the liberal arts as a kind of "finishing school" program to prepare students to join the North American upper class, but as a program in which students may develop their already recognized talents while discovering and nurturing new ones, in preparation for service to others. Because "Culture for Service" is our ideal, we ask students in all our major departments, not just those preparing for traditional "helping" professions such as teaching or nursing, to consider how they might serve others in their chosen fields. We believe this service emphasis contributes to a campus atmosphere which supports and affirms service to others and stimulates a more mature, fully developed examination of what servanthood means in our society.

Of course, one academic department in which the question of servanthood is examined continuously is the teacher-education program. The program operates under the guidance of a philosophy first written in the 1970s and revised during the 1986-87 school year. Among the points of this carefully enunciated philosophy most relevant to this discussion are:

- Teacher education is a function of the entire college.
- Students in teacher education need essentially the same pattern of courses in general education as do students in any other curriculum.
- Teacher education is not a scattered miscellany of courses required for graduation or certification, but a broad and integrally related experience leading to a fully prepared professional teacher.

The stated goals and purposes of teacher education at Goshen College:

GOSHEN COLLEGE LIBRARY
GOSHEN, INDIANA

Goshen College seeks to graduate teachers who . . .

- See the gifts and potential for growth and learning in all students.
- Sense a strong call to serve and to care others with patience and humor.
- Make learning meaningful and connected to students' lives.
- Communicate effectively in writing and speaking.
- Have broad general knowledge.
- Have a broad understanding of the diversity among students and the ways in which they learn.
- Have a solid background knowledge in subjects to be taught.
- Can manage a classroom effectively and considerately, on the basis of the principles of nonviolence, even in difficult settings.
- Nurture human capacities of care, concern and commitment necessary to exercise global responsibility.[3]

Even with such a well-articulated and thoughtful philosophical base, the Goshen College faculty has had to deal with the harsh spotlight thrown on teacher education, beginning in the Reagan administration. Nationwide, conscientious professionals have examined and continue to examine the many issues raised in various reports. However, the excessively negative tone of many of the reports is an annoyance to those toiling in the field of teacher education and a hindrance to genuine improvement. Some of the reports seem to assume that no institution of higher education in the United States is educating prospective teachers effectively.

One such report is *Tomorrow's Teachers: A Report of the Holmes Group*, a group of deans of schools of education. Deans from major state universities dominated the Holmes Group's executive board; the universities involved were described in the group's report as "institutions that attract more than their share of the best and the brightest students; they have the faculty who, on the whole, are the nation's best and most authoritative sources of information in their fields; they command substantial resources; and, in the case of education, they are the institutions that have and will continue to educate the professoriate in education."[4]

In August 1986, 88 deans attended a Holmes Group conference at Wingspread, the Johnson Foundation's conference center at Racine, Wisconsin. Carl F. Berger, dean of the University of Michigan School of Education, reported in a newsletter that the groups planned to address four themes in the coming year. Among them were the group's influencing "undergraduate education so that future teachers will experience a well-rounded [liberal-arts] curriculum in mathematics, science, humanities, reading, writing, literature and the arts," redesigning teacher-education programs "to address basic issues involving the quality and quantity of courses needed by future teachers," and to develop an "ongoing professional relationship . . . with selected schools to enhance the preparation and continuing education of teachers."[5]

I invite the reader to compare these "themes" with the stated goals and purposes of teacher education at Goshen College. As one GC faculty member commented, "Much of what the Holmes Group advocates is already happening in the liberal-arts colleges."

While the Holmes Group seems intent on teaching the elephantine schools of education new tricks, the group overlooks completely the fact that the mouse at the elephant's feet might be a better teacher than another elephant. For instance, liberal-arts colleges are perhaps "the best and most authoritative sources of information" on how to give students a well-rounded education. Similarly, Goshen College and many other liberal-arts colleges require fewer professional education courses already than state university schools of education and maintain close ties with local school systems.

With the help of the teacher-education faculty at Goshen College and current and former students, I have extracted eight qualities that characterize the Goshen College program and are shared by effective teacher-education programs elsewhere.

1. Effective teacher education integrates content and method. GC professors practice "stranding," weaving strands of methods into content courses. Rather than creating entirely

new courses to teach new methods or topics, such as computer use, classroom-management and discipline techniques, or peace education, the Goshen College faculty weaves them into the content courses. The faculty also tries to mold courses to help students deal with problems that may arise in their field experiences. Because GC professors plan together, "stranding" is possible.

2. Effective teacher education integrates the profession with the rest of the college. GC teacher-education students can participate in a spring internship program at the Merry Lea Environmental Learning Center of Goshen College, Wolf Lake, Indiana, an 1100-acre nature preserve. They are trained as field guides and work with approximately 6,000 visitors, most of them schoolchildren who visit the center in the month of May.

Similarly, GC students may take a marine biology course at the college's Marine Biology Laboratory in Layton, Florida. Education students collect specimens for a teaching unit on marine biology. In one of our foods and nutrition classes, education students asked if they could develop a nutrition unit for the classroom as a part of the course evaluation.

3. Effective education is holistic;the program has coherence for the student.

Because our faculty members received their advanced degrees from large universities, they are familiar with the experience of teacher-education students in the large university. They characterized the experience as one of isolation, with a lack of connections to other schools in the universities. Students are left to make their own connections.

At Goshen College, we are progressing with a program review in which we have attempted to clarify what learning outcomes we wish to produce in our students and how we can integrate these outcomes in all departments. Like the stated goals and purposes of the teacher-education program, the outcomes help us focus on our task while not losing sight of the connections between various disciplines. Departmental goals and purposes help the departments understand their relationship to overall mission of the college. Education faculty members are an integral part of this process.

As a mouse might tell an elephant, scale is also important. Just as the most agile elephant cannot help but break things when it walks, so there are some key elements lost in large-scale teacher-education programs. Some schools of education have as many faculty members as GC has on its entire faculty.

Scale is important because teaching involves relating to people in a very special and purposeful way. Teacher-education students must not only be committed to teaching but also to learning interpersonal skills. In a program like Goshen's, professors know their students personally and serve as role models for them. There is continuity because students are likely to have a professor for more than one class. The GC faculty members place students in student-teaching assignments with an eye towards matching the student with a supervisory teacher who can help that student build on individual strengths and improve weaknesses. The faculty members also help students search for their first teaching jobs and provide recommendations themselves; the task is not delegated to graduate students.

One student noted that Goshen College practices what it preaches: the teacher-education faculty not only teaches a model of education that includes sensitivity to learning styles, an emphasis on the importance of each individual and an emphasis on learning from past experiences and building on them, but uses that same model in the classroom.

4. Effective teacher education has professional respect. Not only should the teacher-education faculty have appropriate degrees and pursue research, but the teachers produced by a program should be successful in the classroom.

Much of the success of students is based on their ability, an area in which liberal-arts colleges have an advantage over large state universities. Liberal-arts colleges can be more selective in whom they admit to their teacher-education programs. At GC, the grade-point averages of education students are strong; they are at or above the college's average GPA. Every year, several of the teacher-education graduates are among the top students in their class. For teacher certification, a 2.5 GPA (on a 4.0 scale) is required; students must maintain a 2.8 GPA in their major subject.

After graduation, we expect our students to be professionals, not technicians. Our students are taught to take back responsibility for the materials they use in the classroom. For instance, in reading courses, students are urged to go beyond basal readers and to use reading material with real content and substantive interest and value. "Teachers must share control and be open to discussions of delight and meaning," one faculty member told me. "They must be able to use real books."

One of the gathering places for teacher-education majors is a classroom in which there are several hundred books. There they learn about professional resources they will need after graduation.

Faculty members also are expected to be respected professionals. GC faculty members have served as consultants in Australia, Hawaii, Nova Scotia, South Dakota and in our local area school systems. S. L. Yoder, professor emeritus of education, has given presentations on Goshen College's international-education requirement on both the East and West Coasts and in Denver, Colorado. Faculty members also have held state and national offices in professional organizations.

5. Effective teacher education is multicultural. Even though Mennonite society has traditionally been racially and ethnically homogeneous, the Mennonite Church's beliefs in peace and non-resistance have set Mennonite believers outside society's mainstream. Although Mennonites no longer dress distinctively, we still retain a deep empathy with those whom society considers "outsiders."

Taking into consideration our teacher-education students' backgrounds, we require them to participate in field experiences. For a typical student from a white, middle-class family and a small town, the first field experience takes place in a setting where that student feels comfortable—a school where most students are also white and middle-class.

The next field experience is also in a white setting, but in one where there are more single-parent families and families with lower incomes. The third field experience takes place in a nearby school where most pupils are African-Americans.

The fourth field experience is the Goshen College Study-Service Term. GC requires all students to earn 13 credits in international education. Approximately 80 percent of all GC

51

students earn the credits in the Study-Service Term (SST), a 13-week trimester in a significantly different country. Among the sites where GC sends SST units are Costa Rica, the Dominican Republic, Guadeloupe, Honduras, the German Democratic Republic (East Germany), and the People's Republic of China.

Each unit of 22 students is supervised by a pair of faculty leaders. Students usually spend the first seven weeks in a large city, studying the language, history and culture of the country. They spend the second six weeks on a service assignment, usually in a rural area. Typical service assignments can include working at day-care centers, schools, health-care centers or working with community-development workers.

Students must keep a journal about their experiences. One aspect of SST which particularly affects teacher-education students is that, during SST, the students themselves are put in the position of having to "start over" in learning a new language and new customs.

The SST experience definitely benefits teacher-education students, Professor Yoder believes. "After SST, students can teach more realistically," he said. "They have more rapport with children and they are more resourceful in finding and using materials, because abroad far fewer materials are available to teachers. They also grow in inner resourcefulness and self-confidence."

SST also can benefit faculty leaders. John Smith, professor of education and director of the teacher-education program, recently returned from leading SST units on the French-speaking Caribbean island of Guadeloupe. Like students, the SST leaders gain a new perspective on their culture and their professions.

Goshen College also was the first institution of higher education in the state of Indiana to be accredited by the Indiana State Board of Education to teach TESOL, teaching English to speakers of other languages. Approximately 30 percent of Goshen College's teacher-education students take the three-course TESOL sequence, which is offered in the summer and includes a field-experience segment.

The final field experience before student teaching is an assignment tutoring a child who is having difficulty in school.

Students are encouraged to have a lot of contact with both the child and the child's parents.

6. Effective teacher education is responsive to current classroom realities. Some of those realities are emotional and some are technical. Very early in the teacher-education program, students must actually teach a subject for 10–15 minutes, so that they at least get an idea of what real classrooms are like.

"Classrooms are filled with children who differ from the 'norm'," Anita K. Lapp, assistant professor of education, said. In a classroom, a teacher may encounter students who have been physically or emotionally abused, who are physically challenged, who have learning disabilities, who do not speak English or whose parents abuse drugs or alcohol.

Professor Lapp teaches the GC course on "exceptional" students, an area that is not merely theoretical for her. Last year she worked half time at a mental hospital, teaching children and adolescents who were patients. During the 1986-87 school year, the teacher-education program received a grant to develop a more systematic approach for dealing with exceptional students in the classroom.

On the opposite side of the coin are the fast-moving technological changes affecting classroom instruction. All GC teacher-education students must learn how to use computers effectively in the classroom setting and how to evaluate software.

7. Effective education is richly varied in method. Teaching strategies should promote higher-order thought, reasoning, comprehension, application, synthesis and evaluation. In the GC program, the faculty teaches students techniques of inquiry and discovery, such as using objects and hand-on experiences in instruction, journaling, listening to experienced teachers' stories, and using modern media appropriately. Journaling can be a valuable method to stimulate writing and reading; it can also be a method by which. the teacher-education student can record and analyze experiences.

8. Effective teacher education is an expression of a coherent college mission and educational philosophy.

Many public and secular colleges and universities find it easier to define themselves by what they are not than by what they are. They do not promote or teach any one worldview, be it religious or political. Such a negative description may be the only one possible for certain institutions functioning in the United States. However, one suspects that many complaints about the content of higher education spring from the vague profiles of such institutions.

Because Goshen College is part of a church which has traditionally believed in nonconformity and nonresistance, we can define ourselves by what we believe. GC believes that we offer students a rich and valuable context in which they measure their own horizons and fix their compasses.

In creating that context, we do not disdain our broader world. Goshen College is accredited as a standard four-year college by the North Central Association of Colleges and Secondary Schools; the teacher-education program has been accredited since 1954 by the National Council for Accreditation of Teacher Education and is authorized to prepare teachers by the Indiana State Board of Education.

However, as an institution affiliated with one of the three historic "peace churches," GC also can offer students a different perspective on life. Not only do we have a peace studies program, but the teacher-education program also includes material on how to create an environment in the classroom where mediation and peacemaking skills.

Our outstanding specialist in early-childhood education, Prof. Kathryn Aschliman, is a well-known peace educator and integrates books on peacemaking in the Goshen College Laboratory Kindergarten. Recently the kindergarten celebrated its 30th anniversary with a "Winter Peace Festival," offering displays, videos, and activities to encourage peaceful living for families from the Goshen community.

At Goshen College, "small is beautiful" not just because we are a small college, but because the college is "a community of faith and learning." As the Holmes Group has recognized, teachers cannot be adequately trained in a setting where they study pedagogy only. Neither could they be adequately trained in a setting where they studied faith only. Our effectiveness lies in the intersection of theory and practice, pedagogy and personal example, vision and reality, and faith and learning. No single element could be removed without diminishing the entire program.

Notes

1. Lois Landis Kurawski contributed substantially to this article.

2. Matthew 19–20 (NIV).

3. Goshen College Department of Teacher Education, "Teacher Education at Goshen College."

4. *The Holmes Group, Tomorrow's Teachers: A Report of the Holmes Group,* (1986) East Lansing, p. ix.

5. Berger, Carl F. (1986) "From the dean," *Innovator,* 18 : 2–2.

Participatory Management: A Success Story

Bill Williams[1]
Grand Canyon University

The future prosperity for institutions of higher learning depends on a consensus of management interaction through a participatory environment. As a philosophy, participatory management is "based on the assumption that people prefer to express themselves freely in the work situation, and when they do so, they can be constructive and supportive to others, including their work group and the organization to which they belong."[2] When this philosophy becomes a principle of management, individuals can identify with their work unit, participate in the organization to the maximum extent possible, and therefore should receive equitable rewards. Striving to bring about institutional unity amidst intellectually clashing ideas presents an unusual challenge for a university president. Competence within leadership roles on campus has provided the essential link to participatory management.

At Grand Canyon University, a hierarchial administrative structure establishes the leadership roles on campus. The positions within the structure are commensurate with the authority and responsibility assigned. Participatory management allows the key leaders within the university to become responsible for budget development and expenditure; hiring, supervision and evaluation of personnel; and the establishment of policy and governance within a unit. Supervising these key leaders is a management team comprised of the Vice Presidents.

The articulation of the management team determines the needs of the institution planning and controlling for specific results while stating what it is that needs to be accomplished and by whom. It is the responsibility of those individuals assigned to key leadership roles to perpetuate this articulation throughout their individual units as well as to communicate to the management team as a whole the unit's concerns and suggestions based on the specified goal and mission of the institution. The management system becomes a participative enterprise among administrators, staff, professors and students. Evidence suggest that this kind of enterprise allows individuals to reach their maximum potential, perhaps because the participatory management system recognizes the worth and dignity of each individual.[3] By allowing and actively encouraging all employees to provide significant input into their jobs, they become more involved and committed. As a result, they also become more responsible and accountable for the quality of their job performance and for perpetuating the goals of the institution.

A comparison of research regarding the critical functions of administrators within excellent companies and within effective schools indicates commonalities that the best administrators:

- Communicate goals and mission through personal example and policy development
- Provide support that allows people to perform effectively
- Encourage innovation
- Involve people through collegiality of a "team" approach
- Respond to the needs of the client/public.[4]

One of the goals of the office of President at Grand Canyon University has been to perpetuate the foregoing critical functions throughout all leadership roles on campus. An example of this accomplishment has been the success of the College of Education. It is the view of this President that the success of one college is reflective of the success of the entire institution. That success is the product of a participatory management system which strives to incorporate the critical functions of administrators throughout the university. The following statements are not intended to purport the illusion that all is well, or that there is no room for improvement, but rather to document the ideas and interactions of a system that is "successful."

With the adversity of *A Nation At Risk*[5] and the reports that followed, the Grand Canyon College of Education faculty had to be reflective and evaluative in regard to its teacher education program. Who better to ride the waves of criticism than the faculty and staff directly involved within the College of Education? Participatory management not only relinquishes autocracy but entrusts the selected leadership with the accountability of the results. It was the College of Education faculty that had to determine: What to do? What to change? And—in light of a 95 percent average placement rate for its students—what not to change?

Guarantee Statement

The faculty of the College of Education decided to make a bold statement to the concerned public. What does a business do to market an excellent product and increase customer confidence? They guarantee that product! The College of Education also has an excellent product—a teacher. So, in September 1984, Grand Canyon announced to the community that we would guarantee our education graduates for their first year of teaching. That statement bridged the chasm between community expectations and College of Education realities.

High performance standards are nothing new in the College of Education—they began with the inception of the school itself. The students in the class of a first-year teacher will receive a better education because their teacher has been trained to care for and to meet their individual needs, through curriculum development, delivery of instruction, management of the classroom, and interpersonal skills. With those standards, though, comes accountability—not only for the student, but for the faculty—for it is the faculty who will assist the first-year teacher, free of charge, through telephone conferences, on-site visits, seminars, or additional classes at the college. Faculty accountability, therefore, is a prime expectation at

Grand Canyon. Statements from superintendents, principals and classroom teachers verify that the faculty has produced qualified teacher candidates. Our professors stand behind the education their students have received. Our students, in turn, after completing a rigorous program, feel good about both themselves and their accomplishment. Lastly, the community at large has confidence in the Grand Canyon College of Education, because their children receive instruction from qualified classroom teachers.

What has happened in the past four years as a result of the guarantee statement? Well, many phone calls for advice—but only two requisitions for additional coursework. Grand Canyon also remains the only university in Arizona to consistently offer this warranty to its students.

Student Teacher Residency

In order to better define a "qualified" teacher, the Grand Canyon College of Education began exploring assessment instruments. Feedback to the student teacher regarding teacher effectiveness had not been explicit enough in the past.

Since research on effective teaching yielded data which enabled the profession to identify the competencies effective teachers possess, the Arizona Department of Education developed the Teacher Residency Program Instrument (TRPI). The Grand Canyon College of Education became involved in the use of that assessment instrument in the Spring of 1985. The TRPI incorporates thirty-four competencies assessed through teaching plans and materials, classroom procedures, and interpersonal skills. These assessments have provided explicit indicators of behaviors that a student teacher could employ in the classroom setting. With explicit indicators, the student teacher has been able to change behaviors and become a more proficient entry-level teacher.[6]

As we begin to measure competencies and identify effective teachers, the transition from theory into practice appears to be successful. The Arizona Department of Education received a report from the Maricopa County Teacher Residency Project in June 1988.[7] The data sample included sixty-one teachers who graduated from three in-state universities and several

59

out-of state universities. Even though the sample size is small for 1987–88, preliminary data collected by Enz and Anderson in 1988–89 involving 350 teachers appears to yield replication of the 1987–88 data patterns. Data contained in that report verified what faculty of the Grand Canyon College of Education had first observed in the classroom when using the TRPI: Graduates of the Grand Canyon College of Education performed at a high rate of competency during the assessment observation. Assessing a total of thirty competencies, graduates from Grand Canyon College of Education performed at a higher rate than any of the other graduates on twenty-two of those competencies. The model teaching ability of the College of Education professors has contributed to the tremendous success of our students as beginning teachers.

Experienced Professors

The average number of years spent in the K–12 classroom by our College of Education professors is ten years. They represent a linkage to the community as an educational resource through in-service presentations, leadership roles in professional organizations, and the ability to share their expertise as a model teacher. Grand Canyon College of Education is a practitioner's College. The professors exhibit "excellence" in teaching. A master's degree program was established in 1987 in order to further enhance our status as a practitioner's institution.

Graduate Program

The primary purpose for the establishment of the master's degree program was to provide a learning environment for the professional teacher in which collaborative efforts between the college faculty and the practicing teacher affect the learning of the students in the K–12 classroom. The program is designed to:

- Provide a forum for creative interaction among practitioners

- Promote intellectual growth through coursework and research

- Promote publication opportunities for the practitioners
- Develop a curriculum design that will strengthen the practitioner's academic area.

Evidence of collegiality between the College of Education professors and classroom teachers is presented through collaborative research and publication. Each class session is designed to promote innovative thinking as K–12 teachers strive to meet the needs of the multivarious students within their classrooms.

Curriculum Evaluation

There should be a linkage between academia and the actuality of classroom practice on a consistent and continuing basis. In order to achieve this goal at Grand Canyon University, students, classroom teachers, community leaders, and university professors scrutinized the curriculum for the undergraduate program and the graduate program. The curriculum was adjusted to meet the varying needs of the constituency through the interaction, communication, and advice of all concerned. The College of Education faculty has been responsive to the needs of its constituency through a variety of avenues:

- Suggestions from students brought about curriculum changes and revisions in course requirements.
- The curriculum evaluation conducted by practicing high school classroom teachers brought about substantial changes within the content areas of the College of Business and the Department of Natural Sciences and Mathematics.
- Research conducted by Klopf and Cambra identified specific speaking behaviors typical of the school environment.[8] The speech class on campus did not reflect those speaking behaviors; therefore, a course designed to meet the needs of the classroom teacher was added to the academic curriculum.
- Requirements for the instructional media course were altered, based on the response of a survey completed by

principals, curriculum coordinators, and media center directors.

When classroom teachers in the field assist biology professors and business professors in altering the academic curriculum at the university, there is evidence of participatory management! The input from students, teachers, university professors, College of Education professors, principals, curriculum coordinators, and media center directors is a valuable resource to the teacher education program.

Effective Teacher Education

Effective teacher education is dependent upon high expectations and high standards, from the admission process through the culmination of the student teaching experience. The teacher education program at Grand Canyon University interfaces theory, research, and the world of practice with a strong liberal arts background. Research has documented effective teacher behaviors and it is the responsibility of the teacher education program to verify that entry level teachers possess enough of those behaviors to enter the classroom at a competent level.[9]

The College of Education as a unit can only be as excellent as the individuals who make up the unit. The foregoing examples of "success" were brought about by the culmination of participatory management throughout the unit itself and within the university structure. It is the responsibility of the President to promote the efficiency of one college in order to enhance the unity of the whole institution. The success of the Teacher Education Program should become a prime goal of all universities for it is within that commodity that we hold the future of our nation. All of the scientific inventions, mathematical iterations and technological advancement will be for naught if we are not capable of teaching each and every one of the children of this nation to become a literate, responsible, team worker who will continue learning throughout his lifetime in order to solve the problems of the future.[10]

The Future

The future of America will parallel our ability to educate each and every citizen. In the entire history of the United States, the challenge has never been as great as it is today. By the year 2000, the number of jobs will exceed the number of new entrants into the labor force. Women, minorities, and immigrants will comprise 80% of those new entrants—with the latter two groups traditionally being among the least educated in American society. Historically, that high percentage has never before existed. Jobs of the future will require higher skill levels than those of today. Three out of four jobs will require some education or technical training beyond high school.[11]

"One-third of the forty million school-aged children in the United States are at risk of either failing, dropping out, or falling victim to crime, drugs, teen-age pregnancy, or chronic unemployment. . . . For every two children we educate, we lose one and the consequences are disastrous."[12] If the national graduation rate is 71.1% today, what do these predictions for the job market in the year 2000 imply?[13] Who will be available for the jobs? How will we educate the citizenry to prepare for the year 2000? The answers to those questions could become inherent within the context of the teacher preparation unit and the university as a whole if each and every university accepts the challenge.

It is our experience that a participatory management environment allows for maximizing the potential of the university to fulfill the mandates implicitly placed upon it by society. The university has the intellectual capacity, the "brain-trust," to become the leader for our future world. The university is both the culmination of education and the beginning of education, for it provides opportunities for innovations and for discovering new dimensions of the world both as it exists today and as it will exist in the future.

Notes

1. The author wishes to acknowledge the Dean of the College of Education, Dr. Patty J. Horn, for her contribution in the preparation of this manuscript.

63

2. Taylor, William L. and Cangemi, Joseph P. (1983). "Participative Management and the Sconlon Plan—A Perspective on Its Philosophy and Psychology," *Psychology, A Quarterly Journal of Human Behavior 20*:43–46.

3. Kowalski, Casimir J. and Bryson, J. Richard (1982). "Participatory Management in Organizations of Higher Education: Leadership Mandate for the 80's," *Psychology, A Quarterly Journal of Human Behavior 19*:22–27.

4. Morsink, Catherine (1987). "Critical Functions of the Educational Administrator: Perceptions of Chairpersons and Deans," *Journal of Teacher Education 38*:23–27.

5. National Commission on Excellence in Education (1983). *A Nation At Risk: The Imperative for Educational Reform.* Washington, D.C.: U.S. Department of Education.

6. Horn, Patty J. (1989). "Teacher Empowerment Begins with the College of Education." A Paper presented at the Association of Independent Liberal Arts Colleges for Teacher Education Annual Forum, Indianapolis, Indiana.

7. Enz, B. J. and Anderson, G.W. (1988). "Summary of the Final Report Data for the First Year." (A Report for the Arizona Department of Education, Maricopa County Teacher Residency Project, Phoenix, Arizona.

8. Klopf, Donald W. and Cambra, R. (1983). *Skills for Perspective Teachers* (Honolulu: Englewood Co.

9. Gage, N. L. (1984). "What Do We Know about Teaching Effectiveness?," *Phi Delta Kappan 66*:87–93.

10. *Investing in Our Children* (1985). New York: Committee for Economic Development.

11. *"The Class of 2000"* (1987). A Brochure for Arizona Citizens for Education, Phoenix, Arizona.

12. Perpich, Rudy (1989). "In Education, One-On-One Works," *The Christian Science Monitor.*

13. U.S. Department of Education (1987). *Wall Chart Reports.* Washington, D.C.

Teacher Education: A Vision for the Future

Martha E. Church
Hood College

Nine-year-old Maria skips along to catch her school bus, anticipating what delights the day ahead holds. She's anxious to get to school where she and her classmates will learn about their Mexican heritage. Her teacher, Ms. Martinez, plans to bring to her lesson a rich understanding of how Hispanics live, particularly in America today.

Maria's parents are pleased with the attention she receives and her progress in school. They knew that Maria's chances for learning success would have been difficult without the preschool program available to them. They noticed how her curiosity and personality blossomed under the gentle care and guidance of her preschool teachers.

This year, Maria's parents especially like how Ms. Martinez stimulates her students to learn on their own. "Mama!" Maria frequently exclaims, "I'm through with my homework; can we go to the library now?"

Maria's parents know with steady nurturing her love of learning and curiosity will grow. They even hope that she eventually will become a teacher herself.

At school, Nancy Martinez looks at her excited students and smiles. She was not always sure she wanted to be a teacher. Growing up poor in an inner-city neighborhood, she always thought that if she had the chance to go to college, she would study business so that she could earn a high salary. After making top grades in high school, Nancy received a full scholarship to attend the nearby liberal arts college. There, her professors, particularly in English and biology, inspired her with their own love of teaching about their treasured subjects. Through prodding, encouraging, and challenging, her professors showed how much they cared for her intellectual and personal development.

She knew her friends who attended a large research university were not getting the same kind of support. It was because of her professors' devotion she realized a teacher's mighty responsibility and pure joy in stimulating learning and thinking in human beings.

Nancy's decision to become a teacher was cemented after her first course in the education department. She was taught that *all* children can learn, have the right to attend schools in which they progress and learn, and have the chance to learn equally rigorous content.

Throughout her teacher education program, Nancy was readied for the hard work that awaited her in a school system. Her professors shared the latest in school reform movements and challenged her to think critically about their consequences.

Nancy revisited the desperate conditions of urban schools she had known as a child when she volunteered as a tutor in a nearby city. She studied America's rapid growth of diverse populations and formulated her responses to such change. The latest technology amazed her and she learned how to teach students of all abilities to work with computers. Nancy discovered in the little faces that peered back at her that, clearly, being a teacher meant much more than just teaching.

Today, she stands in front of her eager fourth-graders and starts her lesson. She hopes that her own love of teaching, sparked and fanned many years ago by caring teachers, will someday ignite the same flame in Maria and her classmates.

Nancy Martinez represents the ideal of our teacher education programs in liberal arts colleges throughout the country. Committed to excellence and motivated by a passion for learning, Nancy Martinez serves as a splendid role model for minority and poor children like Maria.

If our future does not hold the promise of thousands of teachers like Nancy Martinez, our education system will be in grave danger, our economic system near collapse, and our children in peril. It is the moral responsibility of liberal arts colleges to reach into our communities, affect change to benefit children, nurture them to become their very best, and convince them that teaching is one of the greatest contributions they can make to American society.

As president of a women's liberal arts college, I see the strides we have been able to make in our own teacher education program. I feel the excitement in our suburban county created by a unique alliance of private and public school educators. I see more changes coming in an already dynamic education system.

By the year 2000, 33 percent of America's school-age population will be minority: blacks, Hispanics, American Indians, and Asian Americans will make up this group. Already in 25 of our largest cities and metropolitan areas, 50 percent or more of our public school students come from minority groups.

Meanwhile, the supply of teachers continues to decline steadily. By 1992, the demand for teachers will hit a high not seen in the last 20 years, and supply will hit an all-time low for the same time period.[1] Further, minorities will make up less than five percent of our teaching force if we allow the present trends to continue.

We cannot change our standards for recruiting and admitting teachers merely to increase sheer numbers. Our schools would be flooded with mediocrity. We know our nation cannot survive amid mediocrity. Instead, we must raise our standards *because* of the challenges that lie ahead for our teachers. Simultaneously, college presidents must work within their communities to do everything in their power to move teacher salaries upward and promote a higher status for teachers.

Classrooms and school structures must allow teachers to work with every one of those diverse children who learn at different paces. Teachers' performance should be evaluated on what kind of progress they make with each and every child.

We need to prepare our teachers to teach a core academic program so our students will be able to think critically and behave ethically. The recent report from the Carnegie Council on Adolescent Development states that our schools need to be small communities for learning where stable and mutually

67

respectful relationships with adults are the basis for intellectual and personal growth.

How best should we prepare those women and men who will teach our children and lead this nation? How do we encourage them to be responsive to changes in teaching methods and learning priorities in years ahead? How will we keep children, especially minority children, in the education pipeline, encourage them to become teachers, and thus, become role models for the next generation? In short, how do we recruit and retain teachers like Nancy Martinez so we can inspire little children like Maria?

A group of top educators in Frederick County, Maryland, recently pondered these very questions and responded by creating an alliance we believe to be unique in the nation. The strengths of five institutions—two private liberal arts colleges (Hood College and Mount St. Mary's College), a community college (Frederick Community College), a state school (Maryland School for the Deaf), and a public school system (Frederick County Public Schools)—were forged to fulfill our moral responsibility to educate our children and meet our citizens' needs.

We could think of no less dramatic a response to ensure Frederick County's future. The Frederick Alliance for Creative Education (FACE) is working to:

- Develop programs for helping at-risk students to complete school, attend college, and become teachers if they so desire;
- Raise the awareness of regional employers of the quality and range of the county's educational opportunities;
- Encourage examination of ethics as part of the educational process;
- Support expanding child-care options; and
- Make the five institutions accessible to all county citizens

This alliance believes strongly in "growing our own" teachers and has taken the first steps in planting its seed corn. We know that we must change to embrace a greater diversity in the students now moving through our education continuum.

At Hood, our liberal arts-trained students will be strongly positioned to be superior teachers. It is because each faculty member believes in every student's worth and her ability to achieve. Just as Nancy Martinez saw in her liberal arts college, our students see good teaching practices throughout the campus, not just in the education department. Our teachers' practices are studied carefully by very critical eyes: How well do they handle the material? Do they inspire learning in class? Are students free to challenge and question?

Although researching and staying active in their chosen field are important to our faculty, teaching is simply what excites them the most. Ever-vigilant about maintaining the highest quality teaching, Hood's faculty embeds problem-solving, critical thinking, writing, and reading skills into solid, valuable subject matter. Additionally, they are open to teaching innovations and recognize that current subjects and methodologies may not be what is required five years from now.

As you can imagine, this kind of attitude prompts some exciting exchanges and learning experiences for both students and teachers.

One fine example is an innovative program of teaching science in elementary schools which, because of its success, is being taught in school districts nationwide by two Hood professors of science education. They show elementary teachers that hands-on experiments and laboratories are more effective in learning concrete science concepts than students reading about science.

Education professor Dean Wood and biologist Paul Hummer began working with the Carroll County, Maryland, school system to refine its elementary science program which emphasizes the hands-on approach. Because of the program's overwhelming success, Carroll County schools received a federal grant to enable Drs. Wood and Hummer to expand the program nationally. The two have traveled across the country training hundreds of science teachers in the new method.

Our students see firsthand from their professors the rewards of new curriculum changes. This, I believe, encourages our education students to ponder new ways of teaching and prepares them in deciding how to propose and implement curriculum changes.

69

As every faculty member in liberal arts colleges is part of that school's teacher education program, then so is every president. Presidents and chancellors have several tasks in our role for improving teacher education.

First and foremost, we need to demonstrate our own commitment to the future by getting involved beyond our halls of learning with groups committed to improving education. My role and activities as a trustee of the Carnegie Foundation signal my very serious concerns for both the students who progress through the education pipeline and those who slip behind or fall out unnoticed. I *have* to find time to be a major spokesperson on education issues—even ones that may make us a bit uncomfortable such as some of our own teaching attitudes and practices. As a brand new trustee of the National Geographic Society, I will be working hard to combat our students' geography illiteracy brought to light by recent reports. As a professional geographer, I have an even deeper commitment to see that this task is accomplished successfully.

No community can afford to lose a whole generation of children. Without involvement and caring that stretches from the president's office to the daily classroom, I fear we may not win the battle of improving education.

Second, in addition to becoming involved with national and local education groups, presidents need to work to improve their own departments and schools of education. One way is to share all the current education reform reports with faculty members, not only in the education departments, but throughout campus. I offer reform reports to our faculty as food for thought without indicating my position on them. This neutrality allows our teachers to decide independently what they would like to share with their students, incorporate into their own teaching practices, or set aside.

Third, presidents need to assign clear and positive value to teaching across our institutions. This means that students see high quality teaching in all their classes. Our students need to develop a rich understanding of a range of disciplines since, as teachers, they will be making these subjects come alive for their own students.

Further, we must fight against steering minority and women students away from math and science courses simply

70

because of a predetermined notion of their interests and abilities. As a women's college, Hood is an ideal setting for helping minorities and women achieve their educational goals. Before arriving on campus, many of our students have felt the subtle discrimination and chilly climate in their high school math and science classrooms simply because they were female.

Our faculty, knowing and understanding the effects of this subtle discriminating, treat every student as an individual with her own special interests and talents. By the simple fact that many of our faculty members are women, our students have excellent role models. Presidents must encourage their faculties to examine the subtle biases toward women and minorities that might still be occurring in their classrooms.

Fourth, we need to work very hard to recruit minorities into teaching careers for the sake of our future generations. Our children, particularly that 30 percent of our future students who will be minorities, *must* see excellent role models who truly care for their well-being and who believe that every single one of them can learn.

I believe that only through these role models will minority children be able to envision their life options and personal success. Without this vision, which is so critical to those students at risk of failing in school, I am convinced our future is in peril.

This year, Hood introduced a set of scholarships that offer half-tuition support to academically promising black students who want to prepare for teaching careers. This scholarship program is buoyed by the wholehearted support of our local schools. Once graduated and certified, says Frederick County superintendent Noel Farmer, these high-ability minority students will receive first preference in employment with Frederick County Public Schools.

Also, Hood, through involvement in FACE, is providing student volunteers to a local elementary school to work one-on-one with first, second, and third-graders. Acting as tutors and mentors, Hood students, who are members of the Black Student Union and Circle K, once trained, meet regularly with the youngsters to work on basic reading skills. The program, if it succeeds in raising the students' performance, will become a county-wide model. I hope that some of these Hood volun-

71

teers will become so excited about their involvement that they will seriously consider teaching careers.

As we have done in Frederick, I believe that every president and chancellor must now find and draw upon their community's resources, inspirations, and commitment to lead America toward its vision for education. We must reach our children long before they enter kindergarten to guide and care for them through early nutrition and preschool programs. We must hold their hands very tightly as they progress through our education pipeline making sure that they do not slip behind or fall out.

Then, our colleges must be ready to embrace these students and their diversities and offer them absolutely the best education in a caring and supportive environment.

I have no doubt that the task that lies ahead of us is monumental. Yet, I also harbor no doubt that all of our classrooms one day will be where teachers like Nancy Martinez work and inspire little ones like Maria to achieve.

Note

1. Carnegie Forum on Education and the Economy. Task Force on Teaching as a Profession, *A Nation Prepared: Teachers for the 21st Century* (1986). New York: Carnegie Corporation.

Ornaments of Society

John H. Jacobson
Hope College

In our generation there is much useful and important discussion of the purpose of a baccalaureate degree and of the purposes of baccalaureate institutions. As we assign due honor to all the claimants for a place within the liberal arts, it is important to remember one basic fact about American liberal arts colleges: That is that many of those colleges aimed initially to prepare their graduates for careers in service-oriented professions. It was assumed that service-oriented professions were fit for liberal arts graduates to enter and also that a liberal arts education provided a significant portion of the preparation for a person to enter a service profession.

Hope College was founded in the 1860s by Calvinist immigrants from the Netherlands who had arrived in Western Michigan starting in 1848. The Holland Academy, a predecessor to the College, had been founded in the early 1850s. In a prospectus of the Holland Academy, the founder indicated the expectation that graduates would go on to college and to careers as ministers, missionaries, or teachers. He also allowed the possibility that some graduates would not enter those professions, but might instead become "ornaments of society." The context makes clear that he both expected and hoped that the ministers, missionaries, and teachers would outnumber the ornaments. In our own day, most college faculties would not be happy if large numbers of their graduates become elementary or secondary school teachers. We hope instead to have students go on to graduate school in the fields

73

in which they have taken their undergraduate majors. Failing that, we hope they will go into lucrative businesses and professions which will enable them to send their children, without financial aid, to their *alma mater* and to contribute generously to the annual fund.

Most people agree that it is important to have excellent elementary and secondary school teachers, but how many of us are as eager to talk about "my son the teacher" as about "my daughter the doctor"? Not all parents are persuaded that teaching is the right route for their own children to follow. A career in teaching is too often perceived as unrewarding in terms of compensation and social prestige.

It is exceedingly unfortunate that teaching is not more highly regarded than it is. Perhaps colleges can do something about remedying that situation. At the very least we can refuse adherence to a value system that assigns high value to wealth, fame, and power and low value to a life of service to others. Just because a profession does not pay well, is not accorded high social prestige, and is not a good springboard to positions of power and influence does not mean that we should turn our students away from it. We may be tempted to think that it would be better if our graduates went into more prestigious and higher paying professions. But it is a temptation we should resist.

Nowadays the cost of a liberal education deters those who are planning a life of service in a low income career. After all, if young people or their families are going to pay out tens of thousands of dollars for a college education, they ought to become doctors or lawyers or brokers and get a decent return on the investment. In other words, if you are going to get a low-priced job, get a low-priced education to go with it. But I really believe that our liberal arts colleges have to assert, here as elsewhere, that there is no very close connection between value and price. The value of a profession is not necessarily commensurate with the price it commands.

Some hold that attention to the practical concerns of a profession like teaching are incompatible with a liberal arts focus. Liberal arts colleges seek to stimulate curiosity as well as practicality in their students. Too narrow a concern for practicality may wall the student off from an interest, a focus of curiosity that might be very compelling if given a chance. Therefore, premature concern with the practical has seemed to be antithetical to the basic values of the liberal arts. The liberal arts address methods of inquiry, presuppositions, values, and underlying theories. Concern with the practical is seen as short-circuiting these intellectual interests and leading in the direction of unreflective technique.

Also there are those who hold that preparation for a profession such as teaching requires professional preparation as opposed to study of the liberal arts. This was the refrain of the conservatives forty years ago when former teacher training institutions were becoming comprehensive colleges or universities. They seriously questioned the value of having future teachers study subjects they would never teach and which did not tell them directly about how to teach. On the other side, our liberal arts colleges maintain that, other things being equal, a better educated person makes a better teacher.

I admit that the inclusion of education within a liberal arts college is of positive value to the liberal arts. The topics addressed in the preparation of teachers are highly relevant to the liberal arts. What different ways have people found to learn and to teach? What approaches best negate handicapping conditions? What other institutions or conditions have an impact on the success or failure of the school? How is schooling approached in cultures other than our own? Some of the most interesting questions in social history, in the social sciences, and in some of the natural sciences come together in the theory and practice of pedagogy. If teacher preparation is conducted by people of intellectual breadth and curiosity, it can be an impetus to, rather than a distraction from, the kind of curiosity the liberal arts build upon.

Liberal education is education to make a living as well as education for living. Whatever may have been the case among the ancient Greeks, in our society liberal education has never been solely for those with leisure to devote full time to public affairs. Most of those who have passed through American liberal arts colleges during the last 350 years have had some kind of career goals in mind. And they have hoped that their education would prepare them in some way for their careers. The connection between education and career is more direct

75

for some than for others. For elementary, secondary, and college teachers the connection is direct. For doctors, lawyers, copy editors, and manual writers it is less direct. It is not so much the specific items of information that are important as it is the methods of inquiry, the skills of communication, the habits of study, and the knowledge of how to prepare oneself to perform a task.

The liberal arts are enriched by a tie to the practical. The study of education within a liberal arts college has value because it reminds us of the fact that, ultimately, practicality is a positive and not a negative feature. That some skill or knowledge is applicable means that it is testable, its mastery can be confirmed in the world of public experience. Unless what we have learned can be, in some way, acted upon, it remains in the realm of dream and fantasy. To know something is to be able to do something. The presence of education within our curricula provides a link to the shared public reality that is so pressing beyond our campuses, and on our campuses as well.

Learning about teaching helps us to be reflective about our own learning, and that is another important reason why the study of teaching is appropriate for inclusion in the liberal arts curriculum. Good teaching about teaching inevitably focuses upon the learner. Therefore as we learn about teaching, what we learn has applicability to ourselves. In examining ourselves as learners, we examine ourselves as persons.

Human beings are able to improve themselves through cultivation and self-discipline, one good form of which is represented by the liberal arts. Teachers exert a positive influence on young people by what they are, as well as by the skills that they display in the classroom. Teachers educated in the liberal arts are important allies to all those who are committed to the value of a liberal arts education. Such teachers are living embodiments of the values we espouse.

The study of liberal arts is important to the prospective teacher. First, it is important as a preparation for living. People need to have a framework of ideas and experiences in terms of which they can understand their own lives and their relations with others. Though often challenged, the framework provided by liberal education is still more satisfactory than that provided by the media, by social movements, or by cult leaders. Liberal education represents the development of a valuable human potential. All students deserve to have that human potential drawn forth.

A liberal education imparts abilities and attitudes that are generally useful, and that are certainly useful to teachers both in their professional lives and as citizens. These include communication, the ability to understand and tolerate people who are different, curiosity, ability to ask and seek answers to questions, and sensitivity to questions of value. What more universally useful and applicable skills are there than the skills of speaking clearly, writing clearly, and thinking clearly, and reading and listening with comprehension.

These skills are at the core of the liberal arts. Through history, the social sciences, and works of imaginative literature, liberal arts students learn that there are cultures other than their own, ways of viewing reality other than their own, and ways of interpreting experience other than their own. This awareness in turn imparts a salutary complexity to their own ways of viewing and interpreting, and also makes them open to understanding how others are viewing and interpreting. As the teacher addresses the needs of pupils from other cultures, other segments of society, families with different experiences and values, the imaginative appropriation of the perspectives of others can be an invaluable instrument.

In former generations, the presidents of liberal arts colleges were much given to emphasizing the fact that education is not exclusively or even mainly for the enjoyment and profit of the person who receives it. They emphasized the obligation of the recipient of education to use that education for the common good. We do not talk that way so much any more. To some degree or other we have bought into the argument that people should go to college because it will enhance their earning power. Also the high prices we now charge have made us less likely to emphasize that the service we sell is a service that is to redound to the benefit of others and not entirely to the benefit of the purchaser. In other words, as a profession we tend to accept consumerist assumptions more than our predecessors did. It is a tendency we should resist.

The presence within our institutions of students preparing for a life of service in teaching testifies to the value we place on the giving of oneself to others. Inclusion of pedagogy in the curriculum is a symbol and a reminder that the college is for those who aspire to a life of service as well as for those who aspire to wealth and power.

Ornamental features of buildings often carry no weight and have no structural purpose. The same is true of ornaments of society. Teachers, on the other hand, do carry weight and are essential elements of the social structure. A master builder devotes as much attention to the beauty and strength of the structural elements as to the ornaments. So should we.

Teacher Preparation, College, and the Real World

H. George Anderson
Luther College

"College is not the real world. High school is the real world." That's what Meryl Streep said, according to one of our recent commencement speakers. From that point on, I left his particular train of thought and began to ponder what Meryl Streep had in mind. She was delightfully right, of course, but why did that statement ring so true?

In the course of the last few months, I've come to consider that quotation as a key to the real world of teacher education. It has offered a host of answers to the question: what are the factors that make teacher education effective? It is surprising that, in the wealth of recent studies on the state of education, effective teacher education is frequently called for, but seldom described. A survey of studies done in the early 80's noted their calls for improvement, but it also showed that none of them defined the qualities needed.[1] A *Nation Prepared* calls for a restructuring of teacher education, but it does not present specific criteria to assess one program against another.[2] Meryl Streep's observation suggests a few ideas beyond the formal studies. Let me jot down a few.

College—at least a liberal arts college—is not the real world because it encourages exploration instead of answers. We create a tent of time for students, giving them four years before we expect them to come out prepared for something. It will never happen again in their lives. We purposely send them off in all directions by requiring courses in various disciplines,

79

often with conflicting methodologies. At our college we further pepper freshman honors students with incentives to attend lectures and concerts in fields that go beyond our curriculum all with the purpose of keeping students from locking in on one field too quickly.

It is this context of exploration that is important for educating teachers. Not only does it stimulate a rich and inquisitive attitude toward life; it also models an openness toward the world that becomes a door to further learning. Students sense that it is o.k. to try something new—that the test won't come until the end of the semester, and in the meantime it's all right to argue with the professor. Somewhere I heard a disease of the mind described as "premature closure." That is another way of talking about jumping to conclusions, accepting stereotypes, and generally acting as though the consideration of alternatives was a sign of weakness. Effective teacher education needs to prop the door open so that educated minds are always slightly ajar.

Another important factor is breadth of knowledge. Here again the liberal arts context proves congenial. Although universities shimmer with the promise of endless variety, the experience of university students is different. A recent study developed a format for evaluating educational institutions on three criteria—breadth, depth and coherence of curriculum.[3] Transcripts of graduates provided data on the courses students actually took, rather than what catalogues offered or majors recommended. The criteria of breadth, depth and coherence were plotted on three axes, so that an institution scoring high on all three scales would be characterized by a cube. Lesser scores would shrink one axis, so that the resulting figure might look more like a slab or a tombstone. The institutions that were surveyed ranged from public research universities to small and inexpensive independent colleges. Liberal arts colleges of all sizes stood among those institutions with broader fronts, indicating that their graduates had taken more than the average number of courses outside their major.

The reason that this breadth is so important in teacher education is that teaching is one of those professions where almost any body of knowledge will find a use. My college employed a high school English teacher to coordinate field experiences for our students in local high schools. "Of course my background in English was especially helpful," he told me, "because communication is such a major part of teaching." He was right, but I expect that in a couple of years some other coordinator will be telling me that her background in Psychology or Management was just the ticket for doing the same job.

Why do insights from so many disciplines prove helpful in teaching? Not only, surely, because elementary and secondary teachers are expected to do so many different tasks—from coaching to advising clubs to organizing field trips. I believe the real need for breadth stems from the fact that teachers up through the secondary level are still dealing with students as persons and not just as minds. In fact many elementary level teachers may have considered the profession precisely because they enjoyed working with children, rather than because of a burning desire to spend the rest of their lives close to mathematics or U.S. history. Working with children means being sensitive to all the interests and problems that beckon or block growth. It is the nature of teaching, therefore, to draw on every skill and insight known to humankind in the ceaseless effort to enlarge horizons and unlock potential. Effective teacher preparation will encourage breadth.

A current discussion on our campus, and probably on many others, centers on the role of academic disciplines vis-a-vis education majors. I understand those who advocate a larger role for the academic departments in preparing teachers. Some would argue that education should be a minor available for those who wish to teach, but who are really majors in English or History or Chemistry. The Holmes Group report also seems to recommend traditional majors during the college years, topped off by a fifth year of professional preparation.[4] My own preference, however, is to avoid the tempting specialization of a major in some discipline. I would rather see the encouragement of a thoughtful selection from a variety of fields in order to prepare future educators for the breadth of challenges that they will face. It is a big mistake to confuse specialization and competence.

The Education department at Luther College has taken an unusual approach to the problem. We have placed the foundation requirements for Education majors in the appropriate academic departments. The specific application of each course to Education is made through special sections or requirements within the parent discipline. Instead of taking Educational Psychology in the Education department, future teachers take our General Psychology course with the usual lab component replaced by our Educational Psychology course taught by psychologists. The same approach works for courses in the history and philosophy of eduction and for fulfilling state requirements in Human Relations. Personnel from History, Philosophy and Sociology integrate these dimensions into survey course sections or into specific electives. The division of labor works well in a faculty where personal interaction is high. Students also get to experience the foundational material from the perspectives of a variety of disciplines rather than through the filter of the Education department alone.

A third factor in effective teacher education is personal development. Some years ago theological education went through an intensive study of the traits that increased or decreased the effectiveness of clergy.[5] Naturally the seminaries and theological schools were betting heavily on Biblical knowledge, preaching skills and counseling ability to be the crucial factors. To everyone's surprise, the make-or-break characteristics proved to be things like "non-defensive integrity" and "loving devotion to people" on the positive side and "impersonalness without trust" and "insecure authoritarianism" on the negative side. In other words effectiveness in ministry relied more on personal character traits than on specific knowledge or skills. I believe the same thing is true in teaching, although probably not to the same degree. However, each year I read a lot of student evaluations of faculty who are up for promotion or tenure, and I note that low-rated teachers sometimes get good marks in categories like "knowledge of subject matter." They are not communicating that subject matter, however; they communicate only that they know it.

The odd thing about post-secondary education is that we officially choose to ignore the personal dimension of a student's life. We seem to assume that the student is already fully formed personally and that the only growth potential left is in the intellect. Listen to faculty talk among themselves, and you will hear comments about students with behavioral or personal problems, but the conclusion will often be, "but she can sure write a good essay." Over in the Student Life office, however, that same student may be the center of a roommate dispute or a disciplinary action. Many of my readers may be saying, "That's not totally true. I personally have spoken to students every year, either at their initiative or at mine, about a mannerism or behavior that is interfering with their performance and their future effectiveness as teachers." Of course it does happen. My point is that it happens outside the assumptions, the job description, of post-secondary education. You are not likely to be fired or denied tenure if you don't do it.

If personal attributes and behavior are critical for success in teaching, and yet the post-secondary environment doesn't assume much responsibility for that area, where do such characteristics get addressed? The short and brutal answer would be: in practice teaching. It is certainly true that many aspiring teachers manage to pass all the tests and get through all the hoops except the last. Their student teaching is a disaster, so they are "weeded out," as the saying goes, before they have a chance to do more damage. But there are other ways, and I believe that they are more likely to work in a liberal arts setting than elsewhere.

One enormously formative influence is dormitory life. Many of our students never had to share a bedroom until they came to college. It's harder to hide at a college than it is at a university, and so students receive a lot of feedback on their behavior whether they want it or not. Another shaping force is the ethos of the college itself. Colleges with religious heritages confront their students with traditions and standards that involve more than personal morality. They challenge students to consider questions of public service, policy and life goals. Finally there is the fact that at smaller institutions faculty inevitably come to know students well, and that relationship can make informal career counseling and comments about lifestyle seem natural. Intentional focus on personal development can thus grow naturally out of the college context. We ought not miss the opportunity.

The first three factors which I have identified as important in the preparation of effective teachers seem especially closely linked with the context of a liberal arts program. The possibilities for exploration, breadth and personal development are particularly rich in the college setting. There are other traits, however, that link more directly to the role of the teacher educator, and in these instances the liberal arts context can be more of a challenge than a help.

It's no secret that Education departments at liberal arts colleges have had to defend themselves and their academic integrity. Other departments tend to wonder if Education is really another discipline or only an application of knowledge which can best be obtained from the "purer" departments. There are historic reasons for this attitude. One member of our Education department remembers his own professors as persons who were undoubtedly excellent elementary and secondary teachers, but who lacked the ability to translate that skill into words and transmit it on the post-secondary and graduate level. "It was intuitive with them," he says. It was like asking a person who has mastered bike-riding to describe it in written form.

Effective preparation of teachers involves a way of thinking and of interpreting data that is distinct from other disciplines. I believe it is just as possible to think *educationally* as it is to think *critically* or *scientifically*. In fact one of the problems with some college professors is that they are only good at practicing the methodology of their own discipline and that they don't know how to teach it to anyone else. Education students who take courses in other departments become accustomed to looking at teaching methods critically. They begin to ask themselves, "How would it be possible to interpret this material more clearly or more openly, so that we would be stimulated to search further?" Actually, they say, "Why is this stuff so boring?", but one question could lead to the other.

I recently read a speech by a statistician who argued that thinking statistically was different from thinking mathematically and that statistical thinking was one of the liberal arts. Fine, but I think it would be much easier to make the case for education and its way of thinking. I would like that line of thinking to become explicit in the preparation of teachers. It is a pre-requisite for their self-understanding and integrity.

Closely related to the need for academic integrity is the need for challenge to the best and brightest students. It is natural for members of other disciplines to urge their most promising English majors or Psychology or History majors to aim for graduate school and an eventual career in research or college teaching. The effect, however, is to counsel these students away from teaching careers at the elementary or secondary level. I don't think this pattern will be easy to change.

Dr. Ed Epperly of our Education Department has proposed an arrangement that might be worth pursuing.[6] Suppose a university that is coming under fire for the poor quality of its teaching assistants could be induced to offer two-year appointments to college graduates—but after the graduates had spent two years in secondary school teaching. In that two-year period the new teacher could begin a graduate program in the summers, so that some course work would be completed by the time the assistantship began. I would imagine that some young teachers would elect to continue teaching as a career, and so the program would produce more than temporary entry-level teachers. The universities would get better-prepared TA's and the schools would get talented teachers. Ultimately, of course, the students who continued through to a graduate degree would bring both academic and practical experience to their future work. That in itself might encourage a closer personal link between secondary and post-secondary levels in the future.

The discussion of employment brings me to another dimension of effective teacher preparation. The future teacher needs to be confident that there is going to be a job out there, and, beyond a job, a career. We have seen the number of entering students who are planning to become teachers rise in the last few years. That upswing reverses a gradual decline going back a decade or more. I can only suppose that the increase reflects the attention being paid to education in the media. The word is getting out that teaching is very important and that the nation needs teachers. The next word that needs to be heard is that teaching is becoming a more attractive career. That message is harder to hear through the debates on certification and salary disputes. We need to interpret these noisy battles as the dawn of a new day and not as an educational Armageddon. Otherwise students will opt for well-travelled paths toward industry or graduate school. Such vocational cheerleading is often frowned upon in liberal arts colleges, but there is certainly nothing wrong with putting one's knowledge to work. Our college mission statement emphasizes service, and the traditional way to serve is through specific vocations. What more honorable path could there be than devoting one's life to the transmission of the best that humanity has learned? If college faculty can't agree to that, then we really will have a problem convincing the rest of society that teachers are worth paying.

These preceding three characteristics of teacher education, academic integrity, challenge, and career potential would probably be readily accepted in the real world. The fact that they are intensely debated in college is one more indication that Meryl Streep was right.

Now I would like to turn to the second half of that opening quotation. In what way is high school the real world? For our purposes we can begin with the fact that high school is one of the field education sites where future teachers encounter the realities of the classroom. I would like to describe a program that we have introduced at Luther College, so that I can complete my list of factors in effective teacher preparation.

In 1987 we were faced with a vacancy in our Education department, and the members of the department proposed a novel solution. Why not use this opportunity to suggest a cooperative program to local high school districts? The college agreed to pay half of the salary and benefits of an experienced teacher in exchange for that person's half-time services over a two-year period. The college refers to this person as "Clinical Professor" and treats the individual as a member of the faculty. The clinical professor teaches a General Methods course to secondary education students for three hours a day at the beginning of their clinical semester, coordinates the clinical semester, and brings in school support personnel (e.g., counselors, administrators, curriculum specialists) and special methods teachers for a related semester-long course. After the students move into their seven-week period of full-time teaching the clinical professor keeps in contact with the supervising teachers, visits the sites, and handles wrap-up and evaluation processes at the end of the semester. The program has been operating long enough for us to have gone through a change of clinical professors, and we are pleased enough with it to contemplate expanding it, with modifications, into our elementary education program.

Our experience with this program has brought me to a couple of conclusions regarding factors in effective teacher preparation. The first is that there is no substitute for reality. No matter how competent our faculty or up-to-date our resources, there is no one more credible than a mentor who "will, that very afternoon, face a secondary class just as they will."[7] Student evaluations gave both the instructors and the General Methods course very high marks. Our college faculty reported, "That was a bit hard on us in the Department since our own past evaluations in similar on-campus courses were much more restrained. The students were never quite sure if we knew what we were talking about . . ."[8] Many states are recognizing this credibility factor and are passing laws that require education faculty to return to the front-line trenches at prescribed intervals. If teacher education is to be effective, it must be credible.

A second discovery from our clinical professorship program has been the importance of strong bonds of respect between the schools and the teaching institution. There is a tendency for schools and colleges to be critical of each other: the schools don't prepare students well, and the colleges don't prepare teachers well. The clinical professorship has enabled our students to learn that "on-campus descriptions are pale imitations of the social reality of a school with its rich interpersonal relationships and administrative structure." On the other hand, school personnel begin to sense the continuum that exists from high school preparation to college preparation to entry back into the high school setting as a teacher. Furthermore, direct contact with local school systems through their own teaching staffs has led to other symbiotic relationships. The college has a program for lending scientific equipment to the schools, and school faculty have become resources for teaching special methods.

College is not the real world. Yet college is the place where we prepare those who are to be trustworthy guides to physical and social reality. That peculiar relationship is not at all bad, in fact it is ideal—provided that the resources of both college and society are employed appropriately to prepare tomorrow's teachers.

Notes

1. Earley, Penelope M. (n.d.). "A Summary of Eleven National Reports on Education and Their Implications for Teacher Education," mimeographed (Washington, D.C.: American Association of Colleges for Teacher Education.

2. Carnegie Forum on Education and the Economy. Task Force on Teaching as a Profession, *A Nation Prepared: Teachers for the 21st Century* (1986). New York: Carnegie Corporation.

3. Zemsky, Robert (1989). *Structure and Coherence: Measuring the Undergraduate Curriculum*. Washington, D.C.: Association of American Colleges, p. 18.

4. The Holmes Group, "Tomorrow's Teachers: A Report of the Holmes Group" (1986). East Lansing, Mich.: The Holmes Group, Inc.

5. Brekke, Milo L., Strommen, Merton P., and Williams, Dorothy L. (1979). *Ten Faces of Ministry*. Minneapolis, Minn.: Augsburg Publishing House, pp. 202–204.

6. A full description and evaluation of the program is in Edgar V. Epperly and Nicholas Preus, "Teacher Empowerment: An unanticipated Benefit from a Clinical Schools Approach to Teacher Education" (Paper delivered at the Third National Forum of AILACTE, Indianapolis, Indiana, June 2–4, 1989).

7. *Ibid.*, p. 3.

8. *Ibid.*, p. 6.

9. *Ibid.*, p. 2.

Learning and the Elementary Teacher

Roland Dille
Moorhead State University

Somewhere in our attic is a book that I sometimes read to our children nearly thirty years ago. *A Day Downtown with Daddy* is about two children, a boy and a girl, standard issue in a book of this sort, who go with their father to his office. There they look at the tall building, the elevator, the outer office, their father's desk. They meet the elevator operator, a secretary, the mail clerk, among others; and they observe a number of simple processes. Everything is sanitized: the floor is clean and the desks are clear; the faces are bland; nothing about the people that they meet suggests that they have lives beyond the office. There is little enough to suggest that they have lives within the office.

I thought of *A Day Downtown with Daddy* not long ago when I picked up a copy of Clarence Day's *Life with Father*, a book I had never read, although I knew that it had been a best seller in the 'thirties and had become a successful play and a much-praised movie in the 'forties. The book begins with "A Holiday with Father," the account of a trip the narrator, as a boy, makes with his father to his office. The author-narrator of this not altogether fictional account of his father takes a good deal of pleasure in his father's idiosyncrasies, pomposities, firmly held opinions, and love, and it is clear that none of these is completely hidden from the narrator as boy. The book is funny, sophisticated in its use of point-of-view, and intended for adults, and it is surely unfair to compare *A Day Downtown with Daddy* with it, but because the exclusion of life and liveliness from *A Day* . . . is not only deliberate but so clearly well-intentioned, one is drawn, after reading a few pages of Clarence Day's book to ask just what is going on. To ask if it is not possible to find a child's equivalent of the richness remembered from the childhood of Day is, it would seem, to be told that, possible or not, it is not preferable. But the young Clarence's questions about the tenements they pass, his curiosity about the tramps they see, and his awareness of how eagerly the young men in the office await his father's departure so that they can smoke do give us a sense of life that we ought not to sacrifice to any theory of the superiority of fact.

A Day Downtown with Daddy was a "Miss Francis" book, that is, a book either commissioned or endorsed by a woman who appeared daily on television, following, as I remember, Captain Kangaroo. In those distant times, when television still felt a tremor of responsibility to something other than its stockholders, Miss Francis was one network's response to the corrupting influence of the violence, the grotesqueries, and just plain silliness of children's cartoons, also broadcast by the networks. Miss Francis, the discovery or creation of television's educational advisers, was a pleasant, somewhat formal woman who explained things, reminding me of what Gertrude Stein said about Pound, "Ezra is a village explainer; all right if you like village explainers; if not, not." She seemed dedicated to absolute factuality, to effects relentlessly following causes, to the celebration of the clear, the plain, and the unmysterious. One had a sneaking suspicion that she disapproved of even Captain Kangaroo's gentle whimsy.

It is useful to remind ourselves of how long some elements of education have countenanced a kind of sterility in the setting of the classroom. An awareness of this is one of the reasons that the question of what a teacher should know, rather than just what a teacher should be able to do has, in the past few years, increasingly engaged the attention of task forces, commissions, and free-standing critics of education. It has not yet earned much attention from those who are responsible for teacher training programs, whose studies continue to show that new teachers are well up on the subjects they teach. It is not hard to see why teachers and their educators continue to focus on teaching practices. The problems of the classroom grow ever more difficult to deal with, reflecting, many of us would agree, the failure of family and community to provide attitudes and expectations that, carried by children into their classrooms, provide the basis for the habits of discipline, attention, and hard work that once, or so we would believe, made the work of the teacher so satisfying. The pleasures of the world, distracting and often destructive, that compete so insidiously with the purposes of the schools, are a part of that same failure.

It is not surprising that solutions to the problems of the classroom have been sought in studies of the nature of children and of learning processes and in experiment with pedagogic practices, for it is there that a great part of any solution must be found. The successful classroom, as described and celebrated by both teacher educators and their critics, is presided over by a teacher who understands children and who has the ingenuity and patience to devise structures and exercises that will involve and challenge pupils.

Classrooms in which pupils are involved in and challenged by a variety of activities are full of the excitement of learning, and we have heard from enough successful teachers to know that such excitement reflects the teachers' own pleasure in knowledge. That such pleasure was made to flourish in a teacher education program is doubtful. The emphasis on theory and practice derives from the certainty that those responsible for teaching theory and supervising practice have about the importance and the usefulness of what they are doing. Those who teach the liberal arts to students in elementary programs are much less convinced of the importance of what they are doing, and might even be embarrassed to hear their efforts described as useful.

We need to rethink the nature of the usefulness of much learning, that is, to regard learning as not only a necessary end but as a means, a kind of pedagogic construct. If we agree that children are naturally curious, that collecting information can have for them the excitements of games, that they enjoy the empowerments of knowledge, then we need to ask ourselves how well our schools respond to these qualities, qualities that ought to guarantee the success of our schools. I know that some

91

will argue that I have described only some children, that most children are just not like that. Well, of course the liveliest minds exhibit the greatest curiosity and get the most pleasure from learning. But there have been plenty of studies that show almost all children who are likely to turn up in our classrooms exhibit these qualities. They are open to experience! And if we say that our schools do a pretty good job, but not a good enough job, in responding to our children's profound interests, it may be because we have forgotten the enticements and excitements of experience, and our children are being robbed of a sense of the richness of the world of learning, because the world of learning has exiled the richness of life.

Remember *A Day Downtown with Daddy*? I am reminded of Diane Ravitch's term, "tot sociology." She had studied the social studies curriculum, and her attention was drawn to the curious nature of social studies in the early grades, which is virtually content-free. Up through the third grade, children study home, family, neighbors, and the local community. That curriculum, now virtually a national fixture, was put into place thirty years before Miss Francis. For all its emphasis on the familiar and the real, it seems to be intensely boring, which is to say irrelevant to children's interests, a gruel too thin to nourish either mind or imagination. It was this tedious exploration of the obvious that took the place, Professor Ravitch points out, of "fairy tales, myths, legends, folklore, heroic adventures, biographies, and history stories."

Children eventually get to history, but here, too, something has gone wrong. A recent report, *American History Textbooks: An Assessment of Quality*, finds that publishers have substituted for the running text "endless photographs, diagrams, charts, boxes, subunits, study exercises, skills applications and so on, especially in lower-grade-level textbooks. The result is that the textual qualities of the history book are reduced to a bloodless subset of a workbook, a mere reading sample by which to test reading comprehension and other practical skills." If they have made textbooks attractive, "this is the attractiveness associated with cereal boxes. . . .

Apparently no one putting together a textbook is free of the responsibility for teaching children to read. Terrill Bell used the phrase "dumbing down" to describe what has happened to textbooks, as content has been distorted or sacrificed in a translation into easier words and simpler sentences.

The enormous problem of teaching reading to children, many from homes where reading and being read to are not part of the daily activities, has put the greatest emphasis on what might be called technical competencies. That some primers, created especially to develop such competencies, are dull should not blind us to the joy a child finds in learning how to read, but the larger excitements that derive from literary merit are lost. There seems to have been some improvement in reading texts and a good many teachers have found ways to supplement the primers with more varied material and to encourage independent reading, but the emphasis on simple skills remains and is likely to be reinforced by the current concern with assessment through testing. Teachers prepared to teach skills, which can, after all, be easily evaluated, are unlikely to recapture for their student their own reading pleasures, even if their educations and the press of responsibilities have left them with such pleasures.

Beyond primers, the next series of basal readers awaits, books, inevitably coupled with workbooks, that again are written for particular purposes, none of them literary. Anyone who suggests that attention should be paid to literary values is likely to be accused of trying to preserve a canon, usually described as white, male, western European, middle class, and conservative. Inevitably some of the books, stories, and poems available even to elementary children will fit that description. Works that have been around for a long time have survived because they are fun to read, but surely we have gone some way toward understanding that culturally diverse classes will provide demeaning and unhappy experiences for some children if the literature assigned is not diverse. By literary values, I mean narration that keeps one eager to find out what happened, characters that can be identified with and that lead us to discoveries about ourselves, an indication that actions have moral dimensions, a celebration of essential humanity, and the pleasures of language, for it is probably language itself that best testifies to the richness of human experience. While no one would prescribe large words for small children, too relentless a substitution of easy words for difficult will destroy

the romance of language, the discovery of the boundless possibilities of words. Nor should pupils need to suffer under the
prosiness of artificial prose. The rhythms of prose like the
rhythms of poetry are filled with intimations of meaning. That
poetry is not often memorized in elementary school is another
impoverishment, for in no other way can the music, which is,
after all, the music of life itself, as easily reveal its magic.

I could argue that some things are more important to know
than others. I do not do so now. If teachers of reading choose
materials that help develop the skills of reading and give
pupils the pleasure of reading success, let there also be someone selecting materials that lead pupils towards the fullness,
the complexities, the richness of life itself, in reading that calls
upon mind and memory and imagination, so that the classroom
becomes endlessly exciting.

How do we educate teachers themselves attuned to the
richness of life? The usual answer has been to require of them
more subject matter. There has been, recently, a good deal of
interest in requiring students to complete a major as well as
the specific teacher education courses. Some have seen this as
best brought off in a five-year program, a year of theory and
practice following a liberal arts education. A variation of this
has been the recruitment of college graduates, who had not
before thought of teaching, into a fast and efficient teacher
preparation program. And still others, a good many others in
fact, believe that the strictly teacher education part of the
curriculum should, in a fifth year, be taught only at institutions
that have the real expertise, that is, that have a faculty made
up of publishing scholars.

There are, I think, two reasons for the call for a major as a
requirement for elementary teachers. General education, plus
a major that allows a student the kind of concentrated attention that is important in an education, is our definition of an
educated person. Second, a student who has majored in a field
is likely to bring to teaching a commitment to learning and a
sense of its excitements. The problem is that a teacher with a
major is likely to teach that major and to leave some other
subjects unattended to. It might be claimed that most of those
other subjects would be provided for by general education
requirements. We have, unhappily, had too much faith in

general education, unwilling to recognize that too wide a selection in our distribution requirement has allowed too many students to choose the inessential and that our major-ridden students no longer take general education seriously.

In fact, it is because our general education does not generally educate that new forms for elementary education need to be found.

I believe that the center of the elementary education program should be a liberal arts requirement, or, at least, a subject-matter requirement amounting to about two-thirds of the work required for graduation: 80 semester credits or 120 quarter credits. This is not unlike one of the options acceptable in California.

I would leave in the curriculum many of the foundation courses but I think that we can forego the argument the history, philosophy, and sociology of education are really liberal arts, it is more important to find ways to teach them more efficiently and in less time. Educational psychology, child development, tests and measurements, and, of course, student teaching, would continue in their traditional ways.

Very early in the program I would require courses in what is usually called human relations, including an introduction to racial diversity, to racism and sexism, to the many faces of bigotry, and the development of an awareness of all those things that can happen in a classroom that are insulting, demeaning, or patronizing. The stereotyping of females needs to be addressed very early in the elementary schools, and students ought to leave the human relations classroom recognizing that that is their responsibility.

All students would get, as they now do, courses that will prepare them to teach art, music, arithmetic, health, and reading. The central liberal arts requirement would have three areas, not of the same size.

First, history, which would include ancient history, American history, including attention to the history of Mexico, Canada, and Central and South America. They will need to know something about Asia, Africa, and the Near East, in courses that might combine geography and culture with history. They will need to know a great deal about Western Europe.

Second, literature, to include poetry, prose, and drama, myths, children's literature, the classics.

Third, science, which should include some basic facts from biology, geology, physics, and chemistry, an understanding of scientific method, a good deal of hands-on experience, in the laboratory and in nature; a consideration of the social and ethical implications of science, and an introduction to ecological problems.

They will also need "bridge" courses that will teach them to move from what they have learned to what elementary students should be taught, and will help them learn how to adapt, organize, and teach such materials, with a good deal of practice in evaluating textbooks. They should learn how to escape from the tyranny of the textbook, how to develop supplementary materials, and how to use a wide range of materials.

Many of the courses in the central core would be those already offered by the college, but there should be no reluctance to develop special courses. Obviously, such courses must demand as much as traditional courses.

Is this a college education? Well, if graduates of this program know more history and geography and more science, if they have read more good books and will continue to read more good books than do our regular graduates, and if they are prepared to take on extraordinarily difficult and useful work, then I don't think that we should worry much about what to call it.

Will the work they take on be less difficult with this kind of education? Surely the program I have outlined is likely to give us graduates committed to learning, excited by the richness of the human experience and by human possibilities. That's a pretty good place from which to begin.

Teacher Education at NCE/NLU— Retrospect and Prospect

Orley R. Herron
National—Louis University

On Saturday, June 9, 1990, at its 104th commencement, National College of Education became National— Louis University. Founded in 1886 by Elizabeth Harrison to assist immigrant mothers and their young children, the College has for more than a century been a part of the Chicago-area educational community dedicated to the preparation of teachers for children, youth and adults. From its initial days on Michigan Avenue in Chicago's Loop to its current educational activities throughout the Chicago metropolitan area and in its academic centers in four states and Germany, the College has linked learning to life through the liberal arts and professional studies. The College has mirrored for more than a century the history of teacher education in the United States. It is from this perspective and as the College's sixth president that I present this view from the top.

In this brief study of a midwest college involved in teacher education throughout the twentieth century, I would like to focus on three themes germane to the art and science of teaching children and youth in our schools. The first theme looks at the relationship of schools to the larger society and the place that teacher education plays in the intersection of the set of schools and society. The second theme addresses the past, present and future practice of teacher education in its efforts to serve both schools and society. The third theme concentrates on the topic of who has, who is, and who will or should teach our children and youth. But first, a brief sketch of the history of the College will provide a backdrop for the views expressed.

Under the leadership and vision of its founder and first president, Elizabeth Harrison, the College was a part of the Chicago Progressive movement dedicated to the betterment of the lives and lifestyle of the urban city. Located in the heart of Chicago, the College addressed the linguistic, intellectual and practical needs of the immigrant and working mothers in a manner designed to promote the fullest possible view of these women about themselves and to convey to their young children this same respect for themselves and others. Central to this vision of the founder was the appropriate and proper education for the young ladies who attended Miss Harrison's Training School in order to prepare to teach young children and work effectively with their mothers. Miss Harrison's Training School became Chicago Kindergarten College and Chicago Kindergarten and Elementary College in successive name changes that reflected the emerging educational focus of the institution.

Edna Dean Baker, alumna of the College, teacher and successor to the presidency, reflected the spirit and commitment of the progressive leaders of the twentieth century's second, third and fourth decades by emphasizing the need for expert professional knowledge and training. The College relocated into its current Evanston, Illinois location in order to link closely with the progressive education movement of the North Shore schools. The College assumed its current name, National College of Education, in 1930, and chose as its sole purpose the education of early childhood and elementary teachers.

The post-World War II leadership of the College was assumed by Dr. K. Richard Johnson, head of the College's science and science education department. Responding to the nation's post-war baby boom, the College became co-educational and added the graduate level to its campus and continuing teacher education programs. The primary thrust of the teacher education program was to strengthen the contribution of the liberal arts in the academic program for the 600 undergraduates enrolled in the College. Dr. Lewis Troyer, Dean of the College,

98

provided the leadership and direction for the "Liberal Arts in Teacher Education" curriculum which was designed to liberate the potential of each student through knowledge and its expression through service to children and youth.

By the 1970s, the baby-boom children and youth had been absorbed by the nation's schools and colleges and the teacher education needs of the nation focused on the increased specialization and knowledge acquired through graduate education and the growing conviction that more needed to be done for young children in and beyond the schools. Dr. Calvin Gross and Dr. Oscar Chute, the College's fourth and fifth presidents, addressed these trends respectively through programs and faculty. In particular, the College reestablished its Chicago roots and opened its Loop center to service undergraduate and graduate needs in teacher education, English language acquisition and the undeserved educational needs of minorities in the city. But, in a sense, the "golden age" for schools, colleges and teacher education that had characterized the fifties and sixties was over. The Vietnam War and the quest for economic, racial and social justice and equity within the nation and especially in our urban centers had captured the central attention of the public and its political and economic leaders. New challenges required new responses from the College and its leadership.

In the summer of 1977, National College's Board of Trustees responded to the economic, educational and organizational challenges facing the College by installing the sixth and current president and embarking on a long-range and strategic planning process led by the president. The result was an expanded mission statement and objectives that reflected the strengths of the faculty, administration and staff in both teaching and the administration and managing of human resources and services within and beyond education and the schools. The complexity of the challenges facing education and the human services increased the demand for research. The doctoral degree was added. The adding of research to the College's continuing commitment to excellence in teaching and service completed the three essential functions—teaching, research and service—that form the central mission of many American universities. The expanded mission statement and objectives resulted in expanded programs and advanced degrees. In turn, the College committed itself to offer its key programs locally, nationally, and internationally. The threefold expansion of mission and objectives, programs and degrees, and academic centers nationally and internationally have resulted in greater enrollments, influence and fiscal stability. This growth has been appropriately symbolized by the College's choice to become National-Louis University at its 1990 June commencement.

Educational scholars, as they view the relationship of the schools to the larger society, whether community, state, or nation, fall largely into two camps. The majority see the schools of any age of culture as a *reflection* of the society they serve. A significant number of scholars, past and present, hold a more active role for schools and hold that schools, properly conducted, can reform society. America's leading educational philosopher, John Dewey, held the major role in this position.[1] More recently, some, including John Gardner, secretary of HEW under President Johnson, would hold that schools *renew* society through ideas and information that renew individuals, who in turn renew institutions, including the schools, which in turn renew the larger society.[2] Each position can probably claim validity, particularly when phrased as follows: for whom, and to what extent, have schools reflected, reformed or renewed society? Each of us can probably answer that question in the affirmative for all three positions for some aspects and outcomes of schooling in our own lives.

The position one takes to this question is vital to the role that teacher education should play in our society. Are teachers the guardian of our cultural heritage, our values, our knowledge and our repertoire of skills? Are these transmitted directly by or through the teacher or are teachers guides to the sources of our heritage, values, knowledge and skills? What role do parents play? Do the media and the community beyond the school door have major roles for good or ill?

Teacher education remains adrift until these questions are answered by society, the schools, or the teacher educators themselves. Dewey's persuasive legacy has left a large part of the American public inclined, consciously or otherwise, to the notion that whenever we encounter a major problem in our society, we turn it over to the schools to organize another course. Lawrence Cremin, professor and past president of Teachers College, Columbia University, has warned us in his recent writings that we have overloaded the school system and its teachers with tasks beyond the time, ability and resources available. His solution is to add an "s" to the teaching profession and declare that in our complex cosmopolitan society we have a number of teaching professions that must collectively and cooperatively carry out the challenge of educating our children, youth and adults.[3]

National College of Education has chosen the Cremin route. The College has and is seeking to increase both the scope and depth of its teacher education program. Increased complexity probably requires both more specialization and more integration of knowledge, skills and learning. It links the knowledge base and skills in each of its teacher education programs directly to the life of the schools in an interactive model. The College, sensing the many forces and social problems that overwhelm the schools and their students, has also moved rapidly to develop concomitant programs in health, human services, the liberal arts and language, and in the development and management of human resources and organizations. Complex problems require complex bodies of knowledge and skills to achieve personal and societal solutions. The primary tension surrounding this task is to balance specialization within and among disciplines and colleges with an overarching integrated view of the individual, the family, community and society. Teachers within the classroom and school must have the time and resources to work directly with students in acquiring the basic skills and knowledge necessary for them to function successfully in life roles as adults. They must make sure the schools provide the level of literacy essential to further learning as adults. A careful analysis must be made of all areas in the school curricula to determine what is to be taught by whom and when. Learning that is not primary to the schools needs to be consciously linked to one or more of the other Cremin teaching professions.

The second theme highlighted in this essay is the practice of teacher education. This encompasses those activities and programs that are customarily linked to the school of education

101

at the university level or to the division or department of education in the liberal arts college. It is related to both the general education offerings and requirements of institutions of higher education as well as the academic disciplines represented largely in the upper level courses at the baccalaureate level.

The history of National College of Education over the past century mirrors the American experience in preparing its teachers, particularly at the elementary level. Its nineteenth century offerings and activities reflected a blend of general knowledge with heavy emphasis on the knowledge and skills necessary to train young children. The first half of the twentieth century developed the professional Bachelor of Education degree with its blend of general education and heavy emphasis on specific content methods and skills needed for understanding the child and successfully managing a classroom. In-depth knowledge of one or more academic areas was missing. The primary thrust at National College during the 1950s was a significant enlargement of the enrollments in the undergraduate Bachelor of Education degree plus the addition of a general Master of Education degree. This master's degree allowed the practicing teacher to complement knowledge and skills needed for current or emerging school programs while linking it to a set of core courses that related to the historical/philosophical/psychological foundations of education. Sputnik, and the scientific, technological and information revolutions of the 1960s focused national attention on the content subjects in the elementary and secondary schools of this country. Teacher education responded by adding the knowledge needed at the college level to comprehend and teach these subjects. National College dropped its Bachelor of Education degree in favor of a Bachelor of Arts degree focusing three-fourths of its four-year program on general education and an upper division major in humanities, behavioral sciences, or science and mathematics. The College's commitment to direct experiences in the schools over the four-year curriculum "Liberal Arts in Teacher Education" forced the elimination of a standard requirement in most liberal arts colleges, foreign language.

The bachelor of arts approach with the blend of general education, a divisional major and professional education courses has served teacher education effectively to the present. The program does not differ much from current recommendations that endorse a certification program at the baccalaureate level.

A second option developed by the College in the early 1970s also anticipated in large measure current recommendations of the Carnegie Commission on Teacher Education and others that four years of general education plus one or more academic disciplines should constitute the baccalaureate degree with professional knowledge and skills reserved to a fifth year. The Master of Arts in Teaching (MAT) provides this experience for certification at the elementary and middle school level. The program meets the State of Illinois approval process and is included in the College's NCATE-approved programs. In a blended series of course work and clinical experiences students build on their baccalaureate degrees and enter the teaching profession by this route. This program continues to grow in enrollments and more students at National College are certified by this program than by the four-year "Liberal Arts in Teacher Education" program.

Many of the current educational reform plans deal largely with "input" factors in teacher education. Whatever the blend of academic knowledge from both general education and the disciplines and the appropriate balance of professional knowledge and experience, each proposal for reform focuses on the means of providing schooling to children and youth. The real focus must be on the learning outcomes that characterize the students. William Spady, while associate director of the National Association of Secondary School Principals, wrote in its *Bulletin* of July 1972 that the "central task of education is to provide (and accomplish) learning outcomes that ensure successful functioning in life roles."[4] This provides a two-part, two-level assessment of education, the first at the level of the schools and the second at the level of an on-going society. Much of education past has assumed that the outcomes set by the school would, in fact, assure successful function in life roles. In a fast-paced, fast-changing technological and information society, the real flaw may well be society's inability to anticipate, delineate and provide the economic, social, civic and occupational roles. In our fast-moving society, political, business, organizational and, yes, even educational leaders are

103

pressured to set and achieve short-term goals at the neglect of longer, often more significant societal and global needs. School systems have been organized in our society to utilize the first two decades of a student's life to enter successfully that third and fourth decades of life. Societal roles, present and future, and school outcomes are irretrievably linked together for good or ill, and the children and youth of today would be better served by both society and its schools if these two essential partners spent more of their limited time, energy and money in cooperative strategic planning for the twenty-first century and less in assigning blame for today's failures.

One other significant fact becomes more apparent to me each passing year. I'm involved in teacher education, higher education, and interacting with leaders and professionals in the public and private schools of this country. For many students, perhaps the majority, the schools *have* provided the learning outcomes that have at least assisted, if not insured, their later success in life roles. In recent years—prompted initially by the able leadership of the former United States Secretary of Education, Terrel Bell, and others—government agencies, foundations, and professional groups and organizations have been recognizing these "pockets of excellence" in American education. Both individuals and schools and school systems have been awarded "Golden Apple" and other appropriate citations and honors. In turn, major and massive research has been focused on these effective classrooms, and to what contributes to this effectiveness. Excellence in education does not need to be discovered, it needs to be transmitted from the existing pockets of excellence to a pattern of excellence throughout our local, state and national school systems.

Dr. Glenn Heck, professor of education at National College of Education and former Provost, draws three conclusions from his participation in, and study of, American education since World War II. First, that the American society and its schools have been largely successful in meeting the *quantitative* needs of children and youth between 1945 and 1975. The nation and its schools absorbed a post-war baby boom that increased enrollments in the schools by 50 percent with all the attendant problems of new buildings, annual bond referenda, and increased budgets and taxes for personnel and nonhuman resources. This occurred simultaneously with the adoption of mass higher education for the majority of our high school graduates, prompted initially by the World War II G.I. Bill. Post-secondary education increased, not by half, but fourfold during these three decades. It took the combined wit, will and wealth of the nation's citizens and educators to meet this quantitative challenge. As a result of these efforts, more Americans attend school more years in elementary, secondary and higher education than ever before in the history of this (or probably any other) nation.

A second conclusion drawn by Dr. Heck is that this exposure of more people to more education, especially higher education, has increased the general public's recognition of and desire for better education for all. This heightened awareness has, in large part, fueled the current desire for excellence in education so essential to the achievement of desired quality of work and life-style.

The third observation of Dr. Heck is just that, an observation, not a conclusion. The *qualitative* goals of American society and its schools could be achieved in the last decade of the twentieth century *if* American citizens, taxpayers, parents and professional educators are willing to devote the same degree of wit, will and wealth to the *qualitative* needs of American education that they devoted to the *quantitative* needs of American education from 1945–1975. If, perchance, that occurs, it could just be the greatest half-century of educational effort and achievement ever in the history of mankind.

One final theme concludes my thoughts on teacher education as I view it from the top at National College of Education. The age-old question that probably bears more weight for good or ill in teaching and teacher education than any other concerns who is, or should be, teaching our children and youth. Are we getting the best and the brightest as mentors and models for our students? If the test data reported on students in various pre-professional programs are correct, as they appear to be, then the answer is no, at least as measured by academic performance. If not, why not? Equally persuasive data also indicates that we do not value the profession of teaching monetarily, either by entering salaries or by career earnings. Teaching ranks below the midpoint of those occupations considered "professions" in our society on both entering and career compensation. In a complex, cosmopolitan society in rapid change there is a premium placed on the best and the brightest to solve and improve society's economic, health, civic and related needs. It is doubtful that we will solve the nation's educational needs without similar commitments of talent, time and money to the human resources in education. Teaching is not without its talented tenth of professionals. In fact, if a majority or more of students are achieving educational outcomes today that ensure their successful functioning in life roles, then education may well have a talented majority of teachers and professionals now at work in the schools.

Education is the largest numerically of the nation's professions. More than three million professionals teach and staff our schools, colleges and universities. For many of these, the satisfaction of seeing children and youth grow and go on to succeed in life has compensated sufficiently to off-set the imbalance in financial compensation. The decade of the 1990s presents a second "golden moment" to staff America's schools and colleges. Those who joined teaching in that first golden moment following World War II have retired or are now retiring. Those currently being employed, should they choose to remain in teaching as a career, will constitute the large majority of teachers in schools and colleges in A.D. 2020.

The three themes I've addressed related to teacher education are also interrelated. What society chooses, or permits, for life roles in the twenty-first century will affect current and future learning outcomes. How teacher education visualizes the twenty-first century and the programs of education it chooses for its current and prospective professionals will play a major role in setting and achieving the school's learning outcomes. Crucial to both of the above is the talent, time, energy and money that will characterize who is and will be teaching our children and youth. Do we possess as a society and profession, the wit, the will and the wealth to solve the quantitative problems of American education in the decade ahead? From my vantage point at the top of National College of Education and the emerging National-Louis University, I see promising signs. Our expanding, energetic institution is attracting able faculty, staff, and, most significantly, involving students in teacher education programs in increasing numbers in our undergraduate, graduate and advanced programs. As the College has mirrored the past century of teacher education, may National-Louis University be a beacon that attracts the brightest and best to our schools.

Notes

1. Dewey, John (1916). *Democracy and Education*. New York: The Macmillan Co.

2. Gardner, John (1963). *Self-Renewal*. New York: Harper Colophon books; Harper & Row.

3. Cremin, Lawrence (1976). *Traditions of American Education*. New York: Basic Books, Inc.

4. Spady, William (1978). *Bulletin of the National Association of Secondary School Principals*. 10.

Teacher Education at North Park College

David G. Horner
North Park College & Theological Seminary

Introduction

The factors leading to more or less effective teacher education programs at independent liberal arts colleges are numerous; among the most obvious are the quality of students enrolled and the nature of the curriculum students undertake. A less obvious factor, yet one which may become increasingly significant given the pressured operating contexts of private liberal arts colleges in the 1990s, may be termed "strategic fit."

That is, I would argue that the quality of teacher education programs at private liberal arts colleges will be determined in part by the investment made in these programs by institutions. Institutional investment, in turn, should be based on the extent to which the teacher education program "fits" or is close to the center of the institution's overall strategy. The strategic fit will, no doubt, vary from institution to institution, and, therefore, will result in varying qualities of institutional investment and, ultimately, in varying qualities of effectiveness in teacher education programs.

This "view from the top" will briefly articulate the strategic fit of North Park College's teacher education program. In so doing I hope to clarify how issues of strategic fit may be addressed generally and how such rationalizations may influence the nature and effectiveness of teacher education programs at private liberal arts colleges specifically.

Private Higher Education Operating Context and Administrative Responses

American private higher education in the 1980s began to deal with a series of vexing challenges including: demographic decline, dwindling financial aid resources, cost-push inflation, proliferating and incoherent curricula, intensified competition from both private and public sector institutions, ill-prepared students, and scarcity of faculty in popular disciplines (e.g., business and computer science.) As we move into the 1990s there appears to be little relief in sight; indeed, exacerbation of many of these pressures is alarmingly probable. We are forewarned, for example, that the steepest demographic descent is yet to be experienced in the early to mid 1990s. Moreover, demographers point out that not only will the number of 18-21 year olds in the short-run be less but also the ethnic mix will change significantly towards groups (blacks and hispanics) whose higher education attendance rates are lower. Inflation increases in recent months have rekindled fears in some quarters of an unfortunate revisitation of past inflation patterns. And, even if inflation remains relatively low, the federal government's budget deficit and mounting social pressures on government at all levels (e.g., homelessness, drugs, health insurance, environmental pollution) make substantial positive shifts in public support of private higher education unlikely.

As private higher education has attempted to manage its affairs in such turbulent times, recourse to business management techniques have become increasingly popular. Such formerly "foreign" and even offensive terms as "marketing" have become part of the common parlance of higher education administration. This pattern seems certain to continue as boards, administrations and faculties seek effective means of coping with the new phenomenon of "steady state" or actual decline in American higher education.

One business management device which has received reasonably widespread attention in the attempt to develop successful responses to the operating issues facing private higher education is "strategic planning." Early articles appeared in the higher education literature in the mid to late 1970s suggesting how this tool, which was already well established in the curricula of graduate business schools, could be utilized by colleges and universities to chart optimal institutional courses. According to the logic of strategic planning, organizations facing steady state or declining industry environments with multiple competitors, none of which have a dominant "market share," should consider the following specific strategies: "geographical focus," "customer specialization," "product specialization" and "value added".[1] While other strategies are presented in the strategic planning literature (e.g., "leadership," "bare bones/no frills" and "quick divestment"), I mention these specifically because they are at the heart of North Park College's strategic plan and it is with reference to these elements of the institution's plan that the fit of North Park's teacher education program has been assessed.

North Park College's Strategy

The institutional identity of North Park is defined most fundamentally by its sponsorship by The Evangelical Covenant Church. Early after the denomination's founding in America by Swedish immigrants in 1885, a school was established (in 1891) to serve the fledgling church body. The institution evolved over a period of years from an academy, junior college and seminary to its profile since 1958 as an undergraduate liberal arts college (North Park College) and graduate theological seminary (North Park Theological Seminary) sharing a common campus and a common administration.

The ongoing significance of North Park's relationship to The Evangelical Covenant Church can be seen in the following facts: in fall 1988, 50% of the College's traditional undergraduate enrollment (excluding evening and extension education programs) came from the 620 local Evangelical Covenant churches throughout America, and in the fiscal year ending June 30, 1989, of the $3.9 million raised by the institution through its development program more than $2.3 million can be traced to sources affiliated with the sponsoring denomination.[2] The denomination provides a direct annual operating subsidy in excess of $650,000 for the College and the Seminary. It is not surprising, therefore, that as a new administration began in the summer of 1987 and initiated an institution-wide strategic planning process a "specialization by customer" element became an explicit part of North Park College's strategy. Specifically, the plan commits the institution to positioning itself in such a way that it will appeal strongly to the majority of the nearly 100,000 members of The Evangelical Covenant Church as well as to other persons with similar religious convictions.

A second explicit component of North Park College's recently developed institutional strategy incorporates the element of geographical focus. In one sense North Park, unlike many similar private colleges with which it might be compared, is a nationally-based institution in that its primary constituency, The Evangelical Covenant Church, is dispersed throughout the country. Thus, for example, while only two other members of North Park's athletic conference, the College Conference of Illinois and Wisconsin (including Augustana, Illinois Wesleyan, Millikin, Wheaton, North Central, Elmhurst, Carroll and Carthage), draw more than 45% of their students from out of state, 46% of North Park's students come from states other than Illinois.

In other respects, however, North Park is a regional and even local institution. For, if North Park's sponsoring denomination has been its primary defining attribute historically, its location in Chicago has provided a strong second defining characteristic. In fact, in the fall of 1988, 51% of North Park's traditional (full-time, campus-based) undergraduate students reported permanent addresses in Chicago (28.7%) or the surrounding suburbs (22.2%). The strategic implication of these patterns has been the decision to focus institutional attention not only on a particular type of "customer" (i.e., Covenanters and people of similar religious convictions) but also on a geographical location (i.e., Chicago and the surrounding suburbs.)

A third dimension of North Park's overall institutional strategy reflects specialization by "product" or program. From the earliest days of its institutional history, North Park has been committed to teaching both liberal arts subjects and selected professional disciplines. Some of these professional disciplines such as theology and music were explicitly expressive of North Park's church relationship while others such as business reflected the College's conscious attempt to prepare Swedish immigrants and their offspring for involvement in the broader culture.

Because North Park is the only four year, undergraduate college of The Evangelical Covenant Church, it has not cultivated a highly specialized curriculum (e.g. either purely liberal arts or purely professional.) Rather, its curriculum seems to have been based historically, at least implicitly, on the desire to be able to serve as many of the interests and needs of its primary supporting constituency as feasible.

The recent strategic planning process sought to respond to this historic ideal by reaffirming the central role of the liberal arts in the North Park curriculum. Broad, balanced offerings in the liberal arts are regarded as the best, long-term curricular response to the diverse educational needs and interests of a diverse constituency. At the same time the institution's professional education heritage was both acknowledged and affirmed as appropriate to North Park's educational mission as a unique church-related college. The planning process also recognized, however, that while reasonably comprehensive coverage of the liberal arts was realistic, financial constraints necessitated that the commitment to professional education be more selective. Thus, the plan identified five professional areas, consistent with North Park's history, mission and resources, for professional program specialization. The five areas are: church vocations, music, nursing, management, and teacher education. The specific rationales behind these selections will be clarified further in the next section.

Finally, North Park's strategic response incorporates an element of what corporate strategists label "value added"; that is, to add a dimension to the product or service so as to differentiate it from competitive offerings. This area of North Park's plan is the most projective. As of this writing several possible value added initiatives have been discussed but not yet implemented. Some of the ideas under active consideration, however, include: more intentional and elaborate use of the resources of Chicago for freshman orientation, service ministry programs, special academic foci (e.g., urban and ethnic studies), co-operative education, deploying the curriculum so as to provide every graduate with a liberal arts major supplemented by either an area of cognate studies or a second major in a professional discipline, including the feature in some disciplines which have particularly extensive major requirements (e.g., nursing and music) of a tuition-free or deeply tuition discounted fifth year; time shortened graduate degree programs by articulating certain undergraduate majors with the graduate theological seminary, and a distinctive, high profile honors major integrating the traditional Western classics with classics from the Christian tradition on the one hand and emerging complementary and/or critical resources (e.g., Eastern, black, feminist, two-thirds world studies) on the other.

Having taken the time to analyze its history, its mission and its present and prospective operating circumstances, North Park is following the above strategy based on product/program and customer/constituency specialization, geographical focus, and value added features in order to pursue the opportunities and deal with the threats apparent in the 1990s and beyond.

Strategic Fit of North Park's Teacher Education Program

North Park's strategic planning process commits the community not merely to the perpetuation of past programs but to determining the appropriateness of academic and other programs based on their compatibility with the institution's overall strategy as outlined above. The reaffirmation of teacher education through the strategic planning process is based specifically on the belief that this professional program plays particularly well to the customer/constituency and product/program specialization aspects of the North Park plan as well as, although less strongly, to the geographical focus and value added emphases of the plan.

Part of North Park's conscious positioning of the institution to reflect the beliefs and values of its primary constituency, The Evangelical Covenant Church, is reflected in an extensive institutional commitment to personal and social service. Beyond the curriculum this commitment is expressed in the College's support of an expansive "Urban Outreach" program incorporating fifteen separate volunteer student ministries to people in need. More than 40% of North Park's undergraduate students are involved annually in voluntary service in the city of Chicago, such as tutoring elementary school students at Cabrini Green, serving food in soup kitchens, staffing shelters for the homeless, "adopting grandparents" at nearby senior citizen facilities, transporting the elderly to church services, visiting the sick and building houses for the poor. In fact, more North Park students have helped build housing for the needy through Habitat for Humanity than from any other college or university in America. Within the academic program this service orientation is expressed through church vocation majors such as youth ministry and through "helping profession" majors such as nursing and teacher education. Such curricular and co-curricular emphases communicate and reinforce North Park's mission as a church-related college dedicated to Christian witness and service in the world. The teacher education program has historically played a significant role within this service framework.

Second, North Park's teacher education program supports both philosophically and practically the institution's strategy of product/program specialization. Philosophically, as stated above, North Park regards its academic foundation as formed by the liberal arts, in which it seeks broad, balanced coverage. On this foundation five professional areas of specialization are built: church vocations, music, nursing, management and teacher education. The teacher education program is particularly well suited to this structure because it draws so extensively on the College's resources in the liberal arts. Students choosing early childhood education, elementary education or secondary education majors are required not only to complete a general education and professional course sequence but also an additional liberal arts major or double minor.[3] Thus, as a professional program, teacher education at North Park strongly reinforces the College's essential liberal arts character.

But, teacher education does more than support North Park philosophically; it also provides significant financial resources. As a private institution with a limited endowment (just under $9 million at 6/30/89), North Park is heavily dependent on student related revenues (i.e., tuition, room and board) for its operating budget. Given this circumstance, cultivating the proper mix of academic programs is essential. That is, both within the liberal arts and professional disciplines, some programs are high "net cost" and others moderate or low net cost. One short-hand way of viewing the relationship between the revenues and costs associated with various academic programs is to compare the total marginal revenue allocatable to a specific program (computed by multiplying the number of student-majors in the program by the average revenue per student, net of financial aid, board and other variable expenses) with the fixed costs (i.e., faculty salaries, benefits, program expenses, etc.) The net revenue resulting from this analysis represents the academic program's "contribution margin" in support of (or, in the case of a negative contribution margin, adding to the financial burden of) the institution's administrative and other costs.

At North Park, in 1988/89 the average academic program contribution margin was just under 3.0.[4] That is, the average major program at North Park contributed to institutional support a net "surplus" of just under $3 (through the enrollment of student majors) for every $1 spent on the direct expenses related to that program. Academic program contribution margins ranged from slightly negative (e.g. foreign language and chemistry) to a high of just over 9.0 (e.g. speech/communications and business.) The teacher education program contribution margin approached 4.0, making it one of the higher financial net contributors among the institution's academic programs. Thus, both philosophically, through its strong liberal arts basis, and practically, through its cost-effectiveness, the teacher education program fits well North Park's product/program specialization.

The fit of teacher education with the other primary elements of North Park's strategic plan, geographical focus and value added provisions, is positive but less substantial. There is no particular reason to believe, for example, that high school

115

students in Chicago and the surrounding suburbs have an unusually keen interest in careers in teaching. Indeed, the negative publicity given to the Chicago public schools recently probably represents a discouraging factor towards such interest. However, in part because of the critical needs of public education in Illinois at this time, the state has developed some financial aid incentive programs to attract students into teaching. These programs, which underwrite a significant portion of a student's tuition costs in return for a commitment to teaching for a period of years, do. provide incentives which match well North Park's student recruitment focus within Illinois.

Finally, it may well be that as the value added aspects of North Park's strategic plan are clarified in the future specific and substantial value added dimensions of the teacher education program can be developed. At this point, however, such dimensions have not been identified, except the obviously rich resources for student teaching which exist in the inner-city, outer-city and suburban schools convenient to North Park students. These resources support one of the value added themes which has been tentatively identified, namely, the resources of Chicago.

Conclusion

In times of economic constraints, expanding academic interests and intensified competition, private colleges will increasingly need to make tough .choices about the levels of support appropriate to various academic programs. The well publicized decisions within the last year of both Boston University and Northwestern University to eliminate undergraduate nursing programs (despite the national shortage of nurses) reflect the sort of strategic positioning that is likely to continue in the 1990s.

The fate and effectiveness of teacher education programs at private colleges will surely depend in part on the impact of some of these tough choices. At North Park College, reflection on the history, mission and operating context of the institution has led to the development of a comprehensive strategic plan within which teacher education fits well. Such a condition should bode well for the effectiveness of North Park's teacher education program as its strategic significance is recognized and as resources are rationally allocated to support this significance.

Notes

1. Porter, Michael E. *Competitive Strategy. Techniques for Analyzing Industries and Competitors* (1980). New York: The Free Press, p. 190–299.
2. North Park College internal administrative reports.
3. North Park College Catalog (1988/90) p. 114–118.
4. North Park College internal administrative report.

The Liberal-Arts College and the Challenge of Teacher Education

John Brooks Slaughter
Occidental College

Introduction

If you were to ask a group of average American citizens a question about the greenhouse effect, the federal deficit or gene splicing, most would quickly admit insufficient knowledge about those subjects to make a substantive comment. But ask them about the state of our public schools and you will most likely have to end the discussion prematurely because almost everyone is an "expert" when it comes to that subject. Whether parent, taxpayer, business leader, employer, news writer or college professor each of us has a view about our public schools, students, their teachers, administrators and school boards.

Pilloried in the press because their graduates have not achieved as much as or as well as their counterparts in most of the developed countries, because nearly 50 percent of those who began public school have either dropped out or stopped out before graduating, because drugs, alcohol and guns appear to have become nearly as prevalent in school buildings as pencils, paper and books, and because more than 25 million Americans are functionally illiterate, our schools are under considerable pressure to improve.

Certainly there are success stories that have been written about schools that have been improved by adopting new approaches to teaching and learning. The experiments that have been conducted in New Haven, Connecticut, in Columbia, South Carolina, and in Prince Georges County, Maryland, to mention but a few, have demonstrated that reform can take place and can be successful. But replicating these successes on a broad scale has proven difficult. We have heard of a variety of supposedly innovative approaches including "Great Schools," "Effective Schools" and a surfeit of others, all of which have been designed to mobilize the schools and their communities to improve markedly the performance of students and educators in the learning process. And some of these have proved to be effective. We are familiar with magnet schools, talented and gifted clusters, compensatory education programs and alternative schools. Again, each of these models can be said to have a positive impact on a selected but usually narrow population. Even the heralded "Back-to-Basics" movement of the early 1980's failed to have a measurable impact upon the quality of instruction or the quality of learning taking place in our elementary or secondary schools. In the latest national assessments, our students, by and large, still fail to meet expectations in grasping the fundamentals of mathematics, science, reading or English composition. Much is made of the fact that many high-school graduates entering college have difficulty in locating Washington, D.C., on a map of the United States or are unable to pinpoint within a tolerance of plus or minus 50 years the period in which the Civil War occurred.

Teachers and Teaching

Much of the blame for these failures is directed inevitably at the teachers in our public schools. Under siege from all corners, teachers feel the sting of criticism. Some of this faultfinding is no doubt properly directed; much of it is not. Teachers are faulted for failing to maintain discipline in their classrooms, for their supposedly desultory approach to teaching, for being unable to inspire either the gifted or the problem learner, for their inadequacies in coping with the heterogeneity

119

of their pupils, and, even, for seeking pay and workplace improvements. They are blamed for being inadequately prepared to be teachers and for possessing pedagogical skills but insufficient knowledge about the subject matter they are required to teach.

On their part, teachers feel that they have reason to be critical about some things also. Beleaguered, they bemoan the fact that they have to spend more time counseling and dealing with family problems than they have for instructing. Too many of them suffer from burn-out early in their teaching careers and leave the profession in favor of some other line of pursuit. Teachers feel that the large number of administrators and coordinators who form the superstructure of most large school districts absorb more of their time and energy than they assist them in doing their job. They feel that they are underappreciated by the public, that pay increases are approved only grudgingly by politically motivated school boards, and that the environment in which they work is becoming increasingly dangerous and undesirable.

To the extent that teachers and teaching have culpability for the underachievement of our public schools and their students, some of that responsibility must be shouldered by those institutions charged with the preparation of entry-level teachers. The schools and departments of education in our nation's colleges and universities prepare the vast majority of those persons who teach in our schools. In addition, investigative studies about how people learn and what constitutes good teaching is largely the province of such colleges and departments in those higher educational institutions with charters for research and graduate studies. Have these entities failed to fulfill their missions for producing quality teachers or for improving the body of knowledge upon which improvements and reform in public school education can be based? There are many who believe the answer to this question is an affirmative one.

There have been an abundance of studies, conferences and task forces that have examined this issue. Two reports have received considerable attention and generally favorable judgments. *Tomorrow's Teachers: A Report of the Holmes Group* and the report of The Task Force on Teaching as a Profession sponsored by the Carnegie Forum on Education and the Economy, *A Nation Prepared: Teachers for the Twenty-first Century*, both address the matters of teacher preparation and certification and the responsibilities of colleges and universities for those functions. But before identifying and, then, commenting upon some of the recommendations of those reports, it is appropriate to point out one of the sociological truths that seriously hampers many schools and departments of education. Although I have not observed it to be as prevalent in liberal-arts colleges as it is in research universities, the culture in which most education departments or colleges reside is one in which they are accorded a somewhat lesser status by their colleagues in the other units of the institution. This is true whether we are referring to other professional schools in the university or the disciplines in the arts, sciences and the humanities. This *de facto* caste system is understood to exist by all in the university and has a negative impact upon the education faculty as well as present and prospective students. To be sure, it is a form of academic snobbery that dates back to the origins of many colleges as "normal schools" which were considered to be distinctively different from those colleges and universities with a more academic mission. Teaching was seen not so much as a profession but as a vocation. It followed that the schools preparing teachers were seen more as vocational institutions than as places where people were educated. Today, this conflict manifests itself in debates over the quality of the students attracted to teacher-preparation programs, the curricula they study, and the nature of the research conducted by graduate education departments. The issue arises in each of the reports referred to above.

The report of the Holmes Group focuses mainly on a recommendation that a professional career path for teachers be outlined that would assure that any teacher who receives tenure would have satisfied certain requirements for an in-depth understanding of a subject-matter field as well as a fifth-year of graduate work in pedagogy. (Such a requirement is already in place in some states including California.) There would be three levels on the career path: Instructors, Professional Teachers, and Career Professional Teachers. On the first level would be those who have completed their undergraduate preparation but have little, if any, professional training. Professional Teachers and Career Professional Teachers would be expected to have completed either a Master's Degree in Teaching or a doctorate in education, respectively. The report calls for educating prospective teachers by requiring them to major in a core disciplinary area. It proposes that distribution courses be assessed to eliminate the smorgasbord approach so commonplace in many undergraduate curricula and that pedagogy courses be adapted to the specific major of each student. Thus a major in mathematics would receive a different set of methods courses than, say, a student whose major is history. One of the most far-reaching recommendations of the Holmes Group is the one calling for extensive interaction between professional schools of education and the public schools. I will have more to say about this point later.

The Carnegie Report proposed that students receive an undergraduate degree in an arts and science discipline before entering a professional preparation program. This could be in the form of a fifth-year program leading to a Master of Arts in Teaching similar to one of the requirements for the professional clear credential in California. The report also called for the establishment of a National Board for Professional Teaching Standards that would oversee and administer assessment measures to determine the extent to which prospective teachers met mandatory standards. Recertification as a means of requiring teachers to remain current in their field and conversant in methodology was also recommended. Like the Holmes Group report, the Carnegie report calls for increased interaction between teacher preparation programs and the public schools through internships and residencies.

Both reports address the issue that I believe is fundamental to reform in education. That is the recognition that we have been guilty of acting as though education takes place in discrete chunks rather than as a continual process. We must recognize that an effective education should be viewed as a continuum, a seamless web, in which K-12 and, at least, the baccalaureate period are an integral whole. In this way, all segments of education take a responsibility for the whole of the education process and, in so doing, cease to be segmented. For improvements to take place in public school education, the condescension and, even, disdain that is all too prevalent in colleges and universities for much of what constitutes elementary and secondary education must be replaced by involvement and understanding. Furthermore, colleges and universities — and not just their schools of education — must listen to the public schools in order to improve their own programs of study. There should be a greatly increased bilateral flow of information between higher education and the schools as well as interactions between students, faculty and administrators at both levels. Greater familiarity and working together on common goals can do much to eliminate the artificial barriers that are founded on the ignorance, prejudice and "protection of turf" that too often exist. It is fair to point out that the greatest change in thinking and behavior will have to occur in our institutions of higher education. Accustomed to thinking that they rank somewhat higher in the educational pecking order, these institutions must come to the recognition that they are, in fact, interdependent with the public-school systems of the country.

I have long felt that one of the problems encountered by many public-school students is that they view colleges and universities as alien and hostile places up until the time that they actually become college students. This may account for the fact that among many groups, in particular underrepresented minorities, there is little aspiration for a college education. Providing for visits to college campuses for the purposes of using the library, seeing an art exhibit or attending a concert, or simply having a picnic or walking around, can do wonders for removing some of the apprehension. Colleges and universities must begin to show that they really care if they wish to have a positive impact on young learners.

The Role of Liberal Arts Colleges

I believe that there are several opportunities for liberal arts colleges in the foregoing. Generally free of the entrenched bureaucracy that is present in most large universities, the liberal-arts college is able to be more creative and responsive in addressing many of these issues. Since service should be one cornerstone of a quality liberal-arts education, these colleges have a tremendous opportunity, perhaps even an obligation, to make service to our public schools a part of the educational experience of their students and faculty. For example, the Education Department at Occidental College offers freshmen a course which examines the educational process and involves them as tutors and teachers of children with reading problems. Education faculty have also developed a tyro teaching program that places various liberal arts majors — sophomores, juniors and seniors, as well as graduates — in urban classrooms throughout the greater Los Angeles Metropolitan area. Although much less able to institute these innovations on the grand scale that might be attempted by the large, public, state universities, liberal-arts colleges can, nevertheless, mount quality programs that involve faculty and students in public schools or engage public-school teachers and students in the life of their campuses. The results and rewards that can emerge from such efforts improve the education that takes place at both levels. By recognizing and acting upon the interdependency that exists, results can be achieved that heretofore were not present. This is true not only for those liberal arts colleges fortunate enough to have teacher-preparation programs that provide a natural entree to public schools, it is no less true, albeit perhaps more difficult, for those without such programs. But the results justify the expenditure of creative energy required to develop such interactions.

The idea of service as an essential component of a liberal education has considerable merit as one addresses teaching as a profession. Just as we argue that liberal-arts graduates should comprehend and demonstrate the principles of inquiry, literacy, numeracy, history, science, values and the arts, we also should demand that they have an appreciation for the importance of using their education to serve others. As Charles Frankel, the former Chairman of the National Center for the Humanities, put it, "If you have a liberal education, you will live at more than one level. You won't simply respond passively to events and you won't be concerned about them only personally. At least sometimes you see your fate, whatever it is, as an illustration of the human condition and of the destiny of men."

It is my sincere belief that we need to move past the point of proving that our schools don't work or that our teachers are proving to be ineffective and get on with the business of fixing the problems. But this will require fewer arm-chair quarterbacks. Instead, it will demand more people who are willing to become involved in the fray, who are willing to serve. At Occidental College, we meet this goal in part by our elementary and secondary teacher-preparation programs, Upward Bound, Adopt-A-School-in-Los-Angeles program and Math Field Day, to name just a few.

On a more fundamental plane, the liberal-arts college has an opportunity to use its educational mission to eliminate some of the prejudices and stereotypes about teaching and teachers and to make teaching a more valued profession. In the sense that a good liberal-arts education will liberate the mind of the recipient, it is hoped that our colleges will assist students to think critically about education and the ways in which it can be improved.

Liberal-arts colleges advertise themselves as places where students have rare and priceless opportunities to become educated for life, to become educated for living. We promise that a liberal-arts education is one that prepares a person best for living in a world where ambiguities, contradictions and complexities are in abundance. We offer to prepare students for living in this world of conflicts, tensions and confusions and to help them understand that their ultimate success as members of the human race will be measured by their demonstrated ability to transcend these barriers to understanding and harmony. At our idealistic best, we ask them to help create an environment in which people of different nations, races, cultures and religions can share, communicate and build together for the betterment of mankind. We can make greater progress toward these ideals by integrating interactive experiences within the subject matter of our colleges and by requiring specific services of students in our surrounding communities. Enriching and extending college-student experiences in academic life on and off campus provide valuable practice and aid personal value development.

Earlier I mentioned that teachers in public schools, particularly in large, urban settings, have expressed frustration with the demands of contending with classes composed of pupils from a broad spectrum of racial and ethnic backgrounds. The pressures of teaching a group of students who possess many different languages and cultural backgrounds is mystifying to all but the most seasoned teachers.

As America becomes more and more pluralistic in its population mixture, these pressures will mount. Of the approximately 3.5 million students who are entering our public schools each year, the following picture unveils itself:

- 25% are from families living below the federally funded threshold of poverty
- 14% are born of teenage parents
- 15% have definable physical handicaps
- 15% are from families of immigrants
- 15% are from single-parent households (this figure will increase to 40% by the time they reach age 18)
- 10% are from families where the parents are illiterate
- In addition, in most of the major U.S. cities, the enrollment is predominantly students from black, Latino and third-world country backgrounds.

The challenges that these statistics present to teachers is obvious. What we must do to prepare entering teachers to deal with these challenges is not.

The liberal-arts colleges, I contend, have two responsibilities in this regard. One is to assist the pre-service teacher in being able to be effective in the environment in which she/he will teach. The other is to understand that twelve years from now, this "new" cohort will be ready for college, and the colleges need to be ready for them. This latter point is a topic receiving considerable discussion these days.

On the first of these two responsibilities, a true liberal-arts college has by virtue of its mission and curriculum the greatest opportunity in higher education to prepare its graduates for living and working in a society where multiculturalism and diversity are the norms. It is one of the major responsibilities of colleges today and is one in which there is need for and room for much improvement. Teacher education programs in these

126

institutions must become increasingly sensitive to the importance of this issue if sustained improvement of the educational
performance of our public school students is to occur.

Although I have been discussing the advantages and opportunities that small liberal-arts colleges have for teacher education, I would be derelict if I didn't point out one major problem
that if left unchecked could nullify all of these positive attributes. That problem is the high price of tuition and the
associated cost structure of our educational institutions.

We all know that the costs of a quality education are steep.
We also know that most independent liberal-arts colleges have
been required to increase their expenditures on institutionally
provided financial aid because of state and federal-aid policies
that have failed to keep pace with reality. This has created a
serious problem for both students and the institutions. I have
before me, as I write, a thoughtful letter from a student who
has been forced to withdraw from his fifth-year studies in
teacher education because of the inadequate financial aid
available to him. He has determined that his only recourse is
to drop out because all that is available to him is a large
package of loans. He calculates that he would have to earn in
excess of $50,000 per year for the first four years of his teaching
career in order to pay off the debts the loans would create. In
his wildest imagination, he knows that the salary he will be
receiving as a beginning teacher will not approximate this
figure.

Is this an isolated case? I am afraid not. I fear that unless
states and the federal government recognize that their support
to students is far below the levels necessary to address the
mounting need, we are going to find it more and more difficult
to attract young people into preparing to become teachers.
(This will be particularly true if the fifth-year recommendations of the Holmes Group Report are adopted.) The problem
is increasing in size rather than diminishing and requires our
nation to re-examine its public policies about student financial
aid before this dilemma can be solved. While not unique to
independent, liberal-arts colleges, the effects are noted particularly in such institutions because of their sensitivity to
increasing tuition levels and fluctuations in the nation's economy.

127

Conclusion

Liberal-arts colleges are unique institutions in American higher education. Although not the largest producer of teachers for our public-school systems, they make a significant contribution. Their role must become even more important if we are to reverse the downslide in public education and the erosion in confidence that our society has in our schools. Using their inherent strengths to provide their graduates with the intellectual tools and with the will to improve education may be the greatest service they can provide to America's future.

American Education at the Crossroads

Bob R. Agee
Oklahoma Baptist University

Education in the United States stands at a critical cross-roads as it faces the future. Criticism abounds from every quarter citing deficiencies in content; failure to promote character-development; failure to produce an informed, functionally literate workforce; and failure to produce graduates who are able to compete with students from other countries. Leaders of business and industry for over a decade have been expressing concern that a significant percentage of people they hire lack the ability to read simple instructions or work simple mathematical problems. College and university professors have been alarmed at the poor foundations laid at the primary and secondary levels of education that they encounter in their students. Social analysts continue to wring their hands in despair over the rising tide of crime, violence, declining sexual mores, alcohol and drug abuse in the schools. Legislators at both state and federal levels feel the pain and pressure of a frustrated voting public who want something done to correct the problems but no one seems to know where or how to get a handle on what needs to be done.

We have drifted far from the dreams and convictions of those who laid the foundations for the noble experiment called democracy. Jefferson believed that an informed educated public was the key to the survival of a democratic society. His design for the development of a public tax-supported education system represented an effort to see that elementary and secon-

129

dary education was available to all citizens within the republic. Jefferson and others operated with the conviction that people needed a fundamental knowledge base in order to think through issues, make reasoned decisions and choices, and solve personal and societal problems in a responsible manner.

Dewey and others promoted the notion that education was the key to lifting society's sights and aspirations to a higher plain. To be sure there was a time even in the most recent decades when the American public believed that an education was the key to upward mobility. The general public was convinced that the more education a person received the better his or her chances were to move upward in social and economic circumstances. Those who weathered the depression and World War II possessed a great confidence in the value of a high school diploma and most of the adults in that generation dreamed dreams of somehow sending their children to college. The exploding industrial society needed well-educated trainable workers and the blossoming economy offered attractive opportunities and rewards for those who worked hard; applied themselves to learning; and who sought to be honest, responsible, loyal employees. Students in elementary and secondary schools were expected to attain defined levels of learning in order to progress to the next higher grade. Colleges and universities defined the subjects they considered to be minimum foundations for those who would be admitted to higher education. It was assumed that schools existed primarily for the acquisition of knowledge, for the shaping of a sense of appropriate behavior, and for the development of a responsible citizenry. There was some consensus among educators as to what constituted an educated person.

Somewhere along the way the American public has lost confidence in the value of education. There is a prevailing opinion that issues of knowledge acquisition, character development, skill development and functional literacy are secondary considerations for school systems. If there ever was general consensus about what constituted an appropriate knowledge base for all citizens, that consensus has disappeared. The never-ending struggle to get citizens and their legislators to come to grips with funding crises through tax reform or through passing bond issues demonstrates the fading confidence that the American public has in what is happening in schools today. The frequency of calls for reform both from within educational circles and from the general public demonstrates a restlessness and dissatisfaction that runs deep. The flurry of band-aid solutions being proposed from virtually every direction indicates that we are indeed standing at one of the most critical crossroads in the history of American education.

Educators cannot help but ponder two serious questions as we scratch our heads and try to figure out what to do to make our schools the viable attractive value that they once were. At what juncture did our education system begin its change in character and nature and thus begin to lose the confidence of the general public? What can we do to cause the general public to begin to change their opinion about the value of an informed society and allow the schools to again emphasize the acquisition of knowledge, the development of character, and the development of an informed responsible citizenry? The complete answers to the two questions will require the contemplation and perspective of many educators, leaders from a variety of segments of society, and representatives from the general public. The proposals identified below can perhaps serve as catalysts for discussion and hopefully will contribute to our making some helpful decisions about directions to take.

What has contributed to the change in direction and emphasis in our schools that has resulted in the public's loss of confidence in the value of what we are attempting to do? Education in America has been shaped over the past thirty years by four significant forces.

The decision to use the public school arena for experimentation in correcting racial injustice made a significant impact on the character and nature of education in America. Acknowledging that there were parts of the country where racial discrimination was rampant and where large segments of the population were suffering because of that discrimination was a deep embarrassment to a nation which purported to be a free society. As law-makers and the courts began to try to deal responsibly with the question of how to eliminate discrimination against the races it became obvious that the places where desegregation could be forced were limited. They could outlaw racial segregation on public transportation and in public businesses but that would not cause the healthy interaction essential to promoting a free society where all people were treated as equals. The courts could not order desegregation of churches, the second largest congregating group in the U.S. Such an attempt would have been considered an unconstitutional intrusion by the state into the life of the church. The one place under the control of law where legislation could require that people of all races would be expected to participate and interact was the public school system.

Tearing down the walls that shut people off from equal opportunity has been painful in many parts of the country. Strategies imposed by law have resulted in major changes in the way school systems do business. School boards and administrations must operate with great sensitivity to the way that the courts perceive their operation. They have often been handed compliance orders that forced a preoccupation with issues other than learning in the classroom and that forced a channeling of resources into areas other than improving conditions in the classroom. Quite often their anxieties and fears about how their decisions and actions would be viewed by the courts resulted in crippling ambiguity in the operation of the local school. Faculty members, usually unprepared for cross-cultural and interracial interaction, struggled with what to do in the classroom and had difficulty determining what constituted appropriate or acceptable expectations. Parents and students found themselves caught up in tensions and fears that could not help but distract them from the primary purpose of going to school and often students and parents developed a deep resentment toward courts, boards and administrations.

The decision to use the public school system for social experimentation was probably the only way to get society to face up to the injustices and horrors of a segregated society where minorities were forced into patterns of discrimination that robbed whole generations of their potential. That effort at addressing a major area of social injustice, however, has carried with it a price-tag. We have learned that there are limits to what school administrators and teachers can focus their primary energies to accomplish. It is difficult to keep priorities focused on the transmission of knowledge and the development of appropriate behavior and skills when the preoccupation of the entire constituency has been consumed with reaction to other roles being forced upon the school systems. If we are to regain public confidence in the value of education we must find ways to achieve a better balance between our involvement in social experimentation and our commitment to the importance of the acquisition of knowledge as the essential reason for a child's educational experience.

A new dialogue within the educational community could address ways to re-focus our primary energies and concerns on the question of how to produce a more literate and informed society that is at the same sensitive to issues of human justice and responsible freedom. Teacher education programs need to include efforts to engage students in thinking through the purposes and the role of education in producing that kind of citizenry. More attention needs to be given to equipping future teachers to be able to interact more effectively in cross-cultural and multi-racial situations. Student teachers need to come to grips with their role as professional educators in keeping education focused on its dual roles of preserving and propagating knowledge while at the same time producing citizens who are committed to a more just and equitable society.

A second factor contributing to the change in the historic character and nature of American education has been the significant period of emphasis on a free-elective approach to curriculum. In the early sixties educators seemed to reject the notion that there was a body of knowledge that was essential as a foundation for all subsequent learning. It was assumed that every child could pick and choose what he or she wanted to study and could determine his or her own pace of learning. The emphasis on general education faded into virtual non-existence at the elementary, secondary, and post-secondary levels of education. Development of basic skills in reading, proper use of the English language, math, social studies, and the sciences became optional for students. During that period educators promoted the notion that all truth is relative, there are no absolutes, and that it is inappropriate for anyone to define what another person should learn.

The end result of the period of emphasis on a free-elective approach to the educational experience, while a fascinating experiment, has been a loss of consensus as to what constitutes

133

an educated person. At one time educators could define what constituted appropriate general education with some degree of commonality. It was generally understood that there were certain basic foundations that needed to be laid for all subsequent learning. Certain defined skills were needed if a person was to function with any degree of proficiency in the work world and in society. The acquiring of a defined body of knowledge was believed essential to developing a person's analytical thinking skills and decision-making capabilities. There seemed to be basic agreement as to what constituted appropriate behavior for an educated person. The values of honesty, diligence in learning, reverence for human life, respect for the property of others, hard work, and appreciation for the fine arts were considered proper matters to be included in the educational experience.

Somewhere over the past thirty years whatever consensus existed disappeared. The debate over what should be included in general education components of the curriculum and whether that component ought to be required of all students rages at every level. The absence of emphasis on values and on the development of character has contributed to the emergence of a society that can't seem to manage a healthy moral or ethical climate for itself. It is apparent that the fascination with a free-elective approach to education is fading and a new era of effort to emphasize a required general education component has surfaced on the immediate horizon. Teacher education programs need to be engaging their students in research and dialogue concerning what constitutes valid foundations for all learning. Leaders of state systems of education, local boards of education, school administrators, and teachers need to focus substantive thought and energy on developing new definitions of what ought to be included in the common body of knowledge to be instilled in all students. Issues of how to include concern for the development of character and values in order to produce a more responsible society need to be included in the dialogue.

A third force that has impacted the nature and flow of education in the United States has been the spread of the popularity of collective bargaining and the unionization of the teaching profession during the last thirty years. That movement within the teaching profession has contributed to a shift

134

in the nature and functioning of the American education system that has contributed to the diminishing of the public's confidence in what takes place in the classroom. News coverage of strikes and contract negotiations with little clear reference to the specific areas of concern have often triggered negative reactions and feelings within the general public. During the periods of dramatic economic growth within the nation public allocations for education did not keep pace with the annual rates of inflation. Long-standing formulas and strategies for generating funds needed to operate quality education systems and to fund teachers' salaries at levels appropriate to the significance and value of the profession failed to keep pace with need and demand. The shortage of needed funds resulted in over-crowded classrooms, limited instructional supplies, too few textbooks, buildings and equipment that suffer from deferred maintenance, and teachers who were paid terribly inadequate salaries. Collective bargaining and unionization emerged as strategies to call to the attention of the policy makers and the general public just what conditions actually exist in the American classroom.

While the strategy may be a valid approach to addressing the problems and the difficulties, the various publics have not always understood or been sympathetic with actions taken. It seems appropriate, however, to raise the question concerning the point at which the tactics of organized labor can become a counter-productive distraction for the teaching profession. Hershberger's research on job satisfaction and dissatisfaction sheds interesting light on that question.

The teaching profession, as do most helping professions, calls for people who work from a high level of inner motivation. Most good teachers are in the profession out of a sense of caring about people and about the value of education in addressing human need. They seem to function best when they feel good about themselves and their professional role, and they seem to possess a need for challenge to growth and self-expression.

Hershberger used Maslow's hierarchy of needs as a guide to research into the way people respond to their work environment. He concluded that workers indeed were concerned about such issues as salary, safety, security, self-esteem, and self-actualization. He discovered however that when issues of salary, safety, and security were addressed it resulted in some reduction of job dissatisfaction but did not necessarily result in job satisfaction. He referred to these issues as "hygiene factors." Job satisfaction, according to his theory, was a result of addressing the issues of self-esteem and self-actualization. These he referred to as "motivators." The perception of the general public is that union negotiations by the teaching profession are pre-occupied primarily with "hygiene factors." While salary, safety, and security are important contributors to self-esteem they do not produce self-esteem nor self-actualization. Strategies discussed and developed by unions, administrators, and boards must address both "hygiene factors" and "motivators" in order for the profession to rise again to the level of functioning that will command the respect of the general public.

As painful as it may be to admit, the efforts of collective bargaining may have left the impression with the general public that that noble profession called "teaching" is simply one more expression of the "meism" of the 1980s. Admittedly it is extremely difficult to focus primary attention on the cultivation of the intellect and the shaping of the lives of students while at the same time being pre-occupied with personal survival and personal well-being. The time has come for boards, administrators, and classroom teachers to sit down together and acknowledge the mutual blame that all groups share in having contributed to the general loss of confidence on the part of the general public (the voting public). That same conversation should lead to a renewed determination to work together to find ways to recapture our schools for the purposes for which they were established. Hygiene factors are important and boards have the responsibility to see that issues of salary, safety, and security are addressed in sensitive responsible ways. Pre-occupation with these factors only results in further pre-occupation with these factors. Motivator factors are even more essential in becoming an effective teacher and these factors are born from within the teacher. Boards and administrators have a responsibility to look diligently for ways, even in the face of scarce resources, to promote and encourage self-esteem and self-actualization in the life of the teacher in the classroom.

Bob Agee

In 1963, the Supreme Court of the United States issued a ruling which ushered in the fourth major force affecting education in America. In the Abington Township v. Schempp case the Court ruled that holding religious exercises such as prayer and Bible reading in public schools is unconstitutional. The ruling stated that states could not *require* that schools begin each day with readings from the Bible. The brief delivered by Justice Clark contended that there is value to studying comparative religion and the history of religion and even acknowledged the worthwhileness of studying the Bible for its literary and historic qualities. School administrators and the lower courts have reacted to the ruling in the case by excluding any effort to teach moral values or ethical values in the schools for fear of violating the Supreme Court's decision or for fear that someone may file suit against them. The result has been a concerted effort to cast primary and secondary education in a totally value neutral context. Add to that the breakdown in the American family as a teaching force promoting positive values and the stage is set for a society to be set awash in a turbulent sea of valuelessness.

Few decisions by the Supreme Court have sent the shock waves through American education that that one decision did. Fear of being found in violation of the Court's ruling has frozen school boards and administrators into turning their backs on the very roots of many of society's ills. While America has always been a very pluralistic society with multiple perspectives regarding religious beliefs, there has historically been some agreement that the moral and ethical tenets taught by the Bible and propagated by the Judaeo-Christian religious tradition were appropriate foundations for a free and democratic society. Commitments in the Constitution to the sanctity of human life and human property were rooted in teachings in the Bible. The right of every human being to "life, liberty, and the pursuit of happiness" grew out of the general respect for the dignity of mankind promoted in the teachings of Jesus of Nazareth. Concepts of appropriate human relationships, appropriate human behavior, and concepts of home and family were rooted in biblical teachings.

What has been the results of the 1963 Supreme Court ruling and the reaction to it by school boards and administrators? In the first place there has been a general loss of emphasis on

137

character development as part of the educational experience at all levels within public education. There has been a general loss of consensus as to the standard by which we measure and upon which we base teachings about morality, ethics and decency. The loss of a reference point as a standard for determining what is right and what is wrong created an ambiguity in our thinking about how to approach the matter of morality and ethics. Efforts to approach the teaching of values without a credible reference point leads to an "anything goes" relativism. Such virtues as honesty, dependability, thoughtfulness, sensitivity to human need, and responsible behavior have become dinosaurs from another era. Sexual mores have been snubbed as the rantings of religious fanatics while a nation ponders the plague of AIDS, teenage pregnancy, and promiscuity and wonders how it is going to stop the out of control tide. It is time for character development to return to the classroom of our public school systems as a major priority. Teachers, administrators and boards need to think through and develop strategies with parents and community leaders to develop some approach that would enable them to address this critical deficiency in American education.

Conclusion

Education is too vital a part of the great American dream for us to allow it to continue its drift toward ineffectiveness. The public schools along cannot solve the problems generated by the forces identified in the article above. Each event and each force represents a legitimate effort on the part of some segment of society to address problems which were most pressing at the time. Each solution carried with it some negative price tags, price tags which have been largely ignored. The time has come for a new era of dialogue, mutual understanding, creative sensitive thinking, and a new effort on our part to recapture our schools for the purpose for which they were established. Let's make acquisition of knowledge, development of character, development of social responsibility, and the development of a more literate work force the primary aims of education once more. The future of democracy depends on our efforts.

Rediscovering the Teacher

P. Michael Timpane
Teachers College, Columbia University

The 1980s were years of stunning change in the nation's perception of teachers and teaching. It is hard to remember the mood at the beginning of the decade. The 1970s had been a time of great disappointment and discouragement in American education, and much of the blame had fallen on teachers. It was a decade in which the turmoil of desegregation and bussing produced great political conflict surrounding the schools. A "youth culture" flourished and produced a generation gap—remember that? New curricula and notions of open education and other aspects of the romantic movement in American education sprang up and swiftly withered. In the courts and legislatures, the school finance equalization movement affected almost thirty states by the end of the decade, putting new strain on available resources and leading to the backlash of the tax limitation movements in California and many other states and localities.

By the end of the '70s, collective bargaining agreements governed the working arrangements of the great majority of American teachers. As the baby boom turned to bust, the number of openings for teachers plummeted and, as a predictable result, pay levels diminished by almost fifteen percent in real terms during the decade. Schools and colleges of education found themselves with swiftly diminishing enrollments, growing senior and tenured faculties, and weak political and financial support. Many of the reform movements launched during the '70s concentrated mostly upon minimizing or avoiding the perceived shortcomings of teachers rather than building on their strengths; thus we had a quest for teacher-proof curricula and for alternative schools. There was also a relentless press for specialization, whose purpose and effect was to narrow the responsibilities of the classroom teacher. Before the decade had ended, the principal source of federal support for improvement in teaching, the Education Professions Development Act of 1967, had been effectively been dismantled, and its keystone, the Teacher Corps, was being phased out.

Teachers, faced with this onslaught of misfortunes, were increasingly demoralized. "Teacher burnout" became a prominent phenomenon. There was widespread belief that parents and communities had withdrawn their support for schools. At the same time, expectations had risen in a curious sense, as teachers were now expected to succeed with all students—students who were, by historical standards, unruly as social conflicts and altered norms of childrearing became more evident in the classroom. This was a profession in trouble.

One of the most obvious indications of trouble appeared at the points of entry and exit to the profession. Where, at the beginning of the 1970s, one-fourth of the entering college freshmen intended to pursue education as a career, by the early '80s that proportion had diminished to five percent. Among women and minorities, moreover, there had been drastic redirection of talent, as other opportunities beckoned and education became steadily less attractive. The aptitudes of persons intending to enter the profession were, according to the SAT at least, dangerously low—combined verbal and math scores of scarcely 800, itself a decline of almost 100 points over the decade. By the early '80s, fewer than half of education majors had completed the academic (college prep) track in high school, whereas the vast majority had a decade earlier. Turnover in the profession was serious in the initial years—at least thirty-five percent of teachers left the classroom within the first five years, and the higher the recorded aptitude of the teacher the more likely her or his departure. Finally, older teachers, hired in the '50s to educate the baby-boom generation, were nearing retirement age and showing every indication of executing a swift departure at the earliest feasible moment.

The 1980s

Given this backdrop, the most surprising aspect of education reform in the 1980s is that it has rediscovered the teacher. While the many national reports and proposals for reform have contained their share of criticism of the teaching profession, they have nevertheless clearly made teachers an essential part of the solution. They have assumed that teachers could improve their performance and become more effective, and indeed have come to the important if obvious realization that no improvement in educational outcomes of students is likely without more effective teaching. Along with new curriculum requirements and standards, the explosion of school improvement strategies, and the development of accountability programs, the "teacher professionalization project" has become one of the principal legs of educational reform in the 1980s.

As the 1980s end, we observe the reversal of many of the dismal trends of the '70s. During the '80s, for example, teachers' pay has risen twenty-five to thirty-five percent in real terms. Regard for teaching is also rising, in the attitudes reported in Gallup polls and equally significantly in reports from college campuses and from people seeking escape from other professions. The proportions of undergraduates intending to pursue careers in education has been rising steadily from the low point of five percent until it is about ten percent today. A considerable part of the new interest is occurring in the most prestigious liberal arts campuses. There is a similar discernible interest in education as a second career among workers in their '30s, who avoided the profession during its dark days, and among retirees and early retirees in their mid '50s seeking a second career. The "professionalization project" has put forth a series of initiatives designed to enhance the status and performance of teachers—ranging from proposals for merit and incentive pay, to master teacher and mentor teacher proposals, to career ladders in teaching. It has extended to include the development of new roles for teachers in decision-making in school improvement and now school restructuring proposals.

For schools and colleges of education, these developments have helped produce dramatic, if mostly derivative, proposals for improvement and change. Whether from the Carnegie Forum, from the Holmes Group, from the American Association of Colleges, or from others, there have been emphatic calls for the strengthening of the liberal arts preparation of teachers. There have been similar emphases, though less agreement, on strengthening the pedagogical preparation of teachers, with slow but steady progress toward universal post-baccalaureate professional training of one sort or another. There have been important proposals for the expansion and improvement of clinical aspects of teacher preparation, ranging from the extension of student teaching and internships, to the development of induction programs which would link the teacher preparation institutions with the employing school districts in cooperative programs for professional development throughout the early years of teaching. At the policy level, the trends have been promoted by heightened requirements and accountability. Half the states have raised the required levels of preparation for entrance into teacher training programs. Every state has revised certification requirements, often adding post-graduate components; and the majority of the states have begun recertification programs, which sometimes include testing for teachers already in the classroom. These trends seem sure to continue.

Teachers College Programs

Like most institutions educating teachers, Teachers College has been challenged by the development of the '80s and has been able to respond and participate in the general resurgence of teacher education. The College's circumstances are admittedly distinctive. Its historical role as the founding place of many of the most prominent traditions of scholarship and professional preparation in American education is well known. It has been entirely a graduate school of education, affiliated with a great research university, for several decades.

One of the most important sources of Teachers College's progress in the 1980s has been the marked strengthening and expansion of its basic programs in teacher education. Like many schools and colleges of education, Teachers College has in the past two or three years experienced significant new

142

strength in applications and enrollments, but almost all this expansion has occurred in those areas training people who will be in or close to the classroom—elementary pre-service education, secondary education, counseling, and school psychology. Between the mid-'80s and 1989, enrollments in pre-service programs doubled from one-hundred to two-hundred, and enrollments by in-service teachers seeking their master's also increased.

Equally heartening is the fact that the College has been able to garner significant support from corporations and foundations to encourage excellent new talent, often from new sources, to enter teaching. During the past five years, the College has launched the following:

A Peace Corps Fellows program under which returning Peace Corps volunteers are offered an opportunity to secure a master's degree over two years time at Teachers College. During that time, they are assured of employment as teachers in the New York City public schools, and the College is able, with foundation support, to provide fellowship support. During the 1988-89 academic years, thirty-five fellows in the program came from twenty states and had served in twenty-one Peace Corps countries. Even more important, the majority of the graduates of this program continued to teach for a third year in New York immediately after graduation, and others have enrolled full-time in doctoral programs here and elsewhere. Teachers College has been honored by the Peace Corps for this first-of-a-kind program and is in eager discussions at the moment to help expand such programs to other locales. The Peace Corps believes hundreds, indeed thousands, of returning Peace Corps volunteers, would be eager for such an opportunity.

In 1986, the College was able to launch The Mellon Fellows Program with the support of the Andrew Mellon Foundation. This program strengthens the relationship of Teachers College with liberal arts colleges in order to recruit students and establish a training program designed for them. The program now draws approximately twenty-five students per year out of three to four times that many applicants coming from such colleges as Amherst, Brandeis, Barnard, Bryn Mawr, Haverford, Oberlin, Williams, Columbia, MIT, and many others. The graduates of these programs are showing a similar pattern to that of the returning Peace Corps fellows. Of the first graduating class of eleven, all are now teaching, seven in urban high schools.

Teacher Opportunity Corps. Beginning in 1988, Teachers College was awarded a Teacher Opportunity Corps grant from the State of New York. This program enables the College to enroll twenty-five minority applicants from New York City in teacher preparation at the College. These applicants have typically been temporarily certified or paraprofessional employees of the system and other individuals desiring careers in education but otherwise unable to afford them. The graduates of this program will, by definition almost, teach in New York City schools.

Southern Educational Fund Partnership. For the past two years, Teachers College has been part of a joint endeavor with Albany State College, Bethune-Cookman College, Johnson C. Smith, Tuskegee, Grambling, Xavier, Vanderbilt, and Harvard University, in a long-term effort to strengthen and expand the participation of students attending historically black colleges in the education profession. This program starts with pre-collegiate efforts at localities in the South to tap high-school students' interest in teaching, and continues through support programs in their undergraduate years at the Historically Black Colleges, and intensive exploratory summer workshops at Harvard, Teachers College, and Vanderbilt. The upshot over time should be identification and training of outstanding new additional minority talent for our nation's schools.

Professional Development School. This year and last, Teachers College has been able, with the support of the Ford Foundation, to launch an intensive planning effort with Community District Number Three in Manhattan to develop together a professional development school at an elementary and intermediary school in the upper West Side of Manhattan. Through extensive and difficult but rewarding discussions extending over most of two years, the faculties of the College and the concerned schools have developed a full partnership in the provision of clinical experience for Teachers College degree candidates in teaching, as well as other opportunities to draw the College closer to the schools and expand its opportunities to provide support and assistance to them.

Teacher Education Redesign Project. With support from the Pew Foundation, Teachers College has, within the past year, begun an effort to redesign teacher preparation programs in ways which will be specifically suited and attractive to most important and badly needed new entrants, namely, minority teachers, candidates considering teaching as a second career, and candidates for teaching in mathematics and science, to name a few.

Teachers College is more than a little surprised and greatly heartened to have been able to launch these initiatives, which grow out of its historic strength, but owe their existence equally to the resurgence of interest in teaching which has swept through our society in the late 1980s.

The 1990s

The 1980s were certainly a time of greatly enlarged and enhanced national focus on education—the provision of additional resources and the enactment of new standards and requirements. It has also been the time for the development of many wonderful new ideas for strengthening teaching, improving schools, and doing a better job of preparing teachers, but it has not been a time of great and demonstrable progress in terms of student outcomes. This, I believe, is the great unresolved issue as we sit on the cusp of the '80s and '90s, the concern behind the efforts of the President and the Governors to establish national goals for education. There was, in the '80s, an unspoken and sometimes spoken *quid pro quo*—that additional resources and autonomy will be provided to teachers and schools, if improved student outcomes were forthcoming. This has been a time in which education has slowly come to grips with this imperative, but also a time for education's new monitors, in the public and private sectors, to understand the difficult and time-consuming nature of educational improvement. Nevertheless, the '90s will certainly see a time of reckoning sooner or later.

For teachers and teacher education specifically, there will be several fundamental challenges:

145

1. Minority teachers. In all the resurgence of interest in education, there has not been an accompanying resurgence on the part of minority students intending to enter the field. This is a time bomb in the system, waiting to explode. Already, the proportion of minority teachers in the classroom is plummeting swiftly from about ten percent in the mid-'80s to probably seven or eight percent today, and no more than five percent in a few years. At the same time, the demographic composition of our school students is moving in exactly the opposite direction, from perhaps twenty-five percent in the mid-'80s to thirty-five percent by the end of the '90s. Clearly, we cannot have a more and more culturally diverse student body with a less and less heterogeneous teaching force; and we cannot have an education system whose leadership does not reflect the political and educational aspirations of its beneficiaries.

Minorities have left education because they failed to find in it the assured opportunities promised them there in the days of retrenchment. They have left because they have greater opportunities in other sectors of society and in other professions. All too frequently, capable minority candidates have failed to make it far enough in the system to have such a choice, because of the defeat and discouragement reflected in a declining rates of enrollment in college and continuing high rates of attrition once enrolled. If education in general and teacher education in particular does not make important progress in this issue during the coming decade, other improvements will not count for much. I am heartened by Teachers College's early successes with its Teacher Opportunity Corps and Southern Education Foundation Partnership, as well as by the growing awareness of this issue in corporations and foundations and their correspondingly greater willingness to furnish fellowship support for minorities entering education. But it is far too early to predict any substantial nation-wide long-term progress in this vital area.

2. Impending shortage of teachers. Education will remain on the demographic roller coaster during the 1990s in which student enrollments will begin to rise, as will teacher retirements, but prepared teacher education graduates, coming out of the long and deep decline of the 1980s, will not catch up and provide sufficient newly trained persons for teaching. This will

146

put great pressure on local authorities to revert to historical patterns of response, bending or lowering standards in order to furnish each classroom with a teacher somehow described. On the other hand, it provides opportunity if the public awareness for the need for higher standards remains firm and the new demand for teachers becomes a way to keep salaries steadily rising and ensure vigorous efforts to recruit from new sources or from previously prepared teachers, who have embarked upon other careers.

3. The readiness of teachers to continue participating in reform. One of the most ominous realities at the end of the 1980s is that teachers are ambivalent about proposed reforms and even about the proposed new roles for them. This is understandable in that they were often slighted or ignored in the preparation of the original critiques and reform proposals. Many might prefer to see the restoration and support of the traditional roles they have long held for themselves before being asked to take on new roles and responsibilities.

From the perspective of teacher preparation institutions, if we expect teachers to behave in a markedly different way in respect to school decision-making, curriculum development, pedagogy, and child development, we had certainly better be sure that our training programs have furnished them with the requisite knowledge and skills.

4. Continuing political support. One of the most amazing developments of the 1980s has been the extended period in which education has remained an issue of political and financial priority. There was much talk at the outset of a two year "window of opportunity;" but now, seven years later, the support of the state governments and of the business community seems if anything stronger. Both parties are driven by long-term demographic and economic development considerations, and seem to be developing an important understanding of the requisite need for sustained support if educational improvement is to be achieved.

A welcome new turn is occurring at the national level. The interest of the President and the Governors in setting national goals and standards must be counted auspicious. From the specific perspective of aiding teachers, there are important and ambitious new legislative proposals in Congress to reestablish the Teacher Corps, provide strong incentives to encourage minorities and second-career entrants to join the profession, as well as strengthening teaching in early childhood and for mathematics and science. This kind of support would provide critically needed marginal resources for improvements in teaching and teacher education.

Conclusion

For any institution involved in teacher education, this must be a most exciting and challenging time. Nothing will be handed to us on a platter, and indeed we must in many cases race to catch up with the imperatives of educational reform and improvement, but we have been given every fair chance to do so—challenged but not written off. If we fail to meet this challenge, the deal will not be as attractive the next time around.

About the Contributors and Their Institutions

John T. Dahlquist, Vice President
Arkansas College
PO Box 2317
Batesville, AR 72503-2317

Vice President Dahlquist received his undergraduate education at American University and Boston University. He earned a B.A. degree from the College of Liberal Arts at Boston and continued his work there subsequently earning S.T.B. and Ph.D. degrees. He assumed the role of Acting President of Arkansas College in February, 1989, and continued in that role through August when he returned to his job as Vice President for Academic Services and Dean of the Faculty. He also holds the title of Professor of History at Arkansas, a position that he held previously at Kansas Wesleyan. He has taught at other institutions as an instructor or in part-time roles. Dr. Dahlquist has written articles on notable American women, sabbaticals for administrators, and clergy. He has received several awards from the National Science Foundation and National Endowment for the Humanities.

Arkansas College, founded in 1872, is the oldest continuous independent college in the state. Located in Batesville, its church relationship is formally established in a covenant with a Synod of the Presbyterian Church (USA). According to published materials Arkansas College is committed to effective teaching, flexibility in planning for the changing needs of students and society, and to individually designed methods of instruction and counseling. Service to its students is a top priority. Arkansas' calendar, curriculum, teaching methodology, evaluation system and extra-curricular activities all aim at this goal. The College's mission for the Church is accomplished by ". . . liberating students from their egocentricity, encouraging them to develop deeply held values, forming a caring community with open communication between students, faculty and administrators, and relating the wider world to the campus." Approximately 825 students are enrolled.

Thomas Tredway, President
Augustana College
639 – 38th Street
Rock Island, IL 61201

Thomas Tredway earned a bachelor's degree from Augustana College and a Ph.D. in History from Northwestern University. He became president of his alma mater in 1975 after serving on the History faculty there. Prior to becoming president Tredway took leaves to teach at the Lutheran Theological Seminary in Waterloo, Ontario, and to study in Germany. His publications have centered on history of Christian thought. He has served as a member of the International Theological Commission considering theological and historical questions uniting and dividing the Lutheran and Wesleyan families of churches, he chaired the Lutheran delegation in a dialogue with United States Methodists, and he was a member of the Task Force on Theology for the new Evangelical Lutheran Church in America.

Augustana College, founded in 1860 by Swedish immigrants, has maintained a close relationship with the Augustana Lutheran Church and its historical successors, the Lutheran Church in America and the newly established Evangelical Lutheran Church in America. The College's curriculum has remained quite constant through the years consisting of concentrated study in a major field plus broad general educa-

150

tion requirements. Any changes over the years have been evolutionary due to the proven ability of this model. The College is on record stating that ". . . the primary goal of all [faculty] is good teaching." Approximately 2250 students are enrolled.

Harry E. Smith, President
Austin College
900 N. Grand
Sherman, TX 75091

Harry Smith earned a Bachelor of Arts degree in Philosophy from the University of Texas (Austin), a Bachelor of Divinity from Yale Divinity School, and a Ph.D. from Drew University. He became president of Austin College in 1978. Previously, he had been a faculty member at Yale Divinity School, Executive Director of the Society for Values in Higher Education, Special Assistant to the Chancellor of the University of North Carolina at Chapel Hill, and Presbyterian Campus Chaplain at UNC-Chapel Hill. His publications have included the following topics: Christian faith in higher education, models for campus ministry, and secularization and the university. He has been a member of the advisory Council of the Danforth Foundation Campus Ministry Program, the Editorial Advisory Board of *Educational Record*, the Policy Planning Commission and the Commission on Policy Analysis of the National Institute of Independent Colleges and universities. He has served in several leadership roles in state, regional and national associations of higher education and intercollegiate athletics.

Austin College is a coeducational liberal arts institution founded in 1849. It was the first college in Texas to grant a graduate degree. The College opened in Huntsville in 1850 and moved to Sherman in 1876. Sherman was thought to be a "more promising area" after three yellow fever epidemics, the Civil War years, and challenging economic conditions of the reconstruction period. Individual development is an important goal of the College. Programs emphasize student participation in a wide variety of events and experiences. College publications state that the liberal arts nature of Austin College and its residential environment help to assure the comprehensiveness demanded by total education. Approximately 1250 students are enrolled.

Roger Hull, President
Union College
Schenectady, NY 12308
(formerly President of Beloit College)

Roger Hull received a Bachelor of Arts degree from Dartmouth College, a LL.B. from Yale Law School and LL.M. and S.J.D. degrees from the University of Virginia. He became president of Beloit College in 1981. Prior to that time he was Vice President for Development and Planning and Adjunct Professor of Law at Syracuse University, Special Assistant to the Chairman and Deputy Staff Director of the National Security Council Interagency Task Force on the Law of the Sea, Special Counsel to Governor Linwood Holton of Virginia, and a corporate and securities attorney. His publications have included books and articles on the following topics: the law and Vietnam; Ireland; Taiwan; law of the sea; Nazis and Germany; and Nicaragua. Regarding education he has written about the university as corporation, cancellable student loans, foreign language programs, and helping minorities help themselves. President Hull has been a member of the American Bar Association, the American Council on Education, American Society of International Law, Chicago Council on Foreign Relations, Board of Visitors of the College of William and Mary, and other organizations.

Founded by New Englanders and influenced by Yale's curriculum, the charter to establish Beloit College was enacted into law by the Territory of Wisconsin in 1846. From its beginning, the College embraced both a classical tradition and a penchant for innovation and experimentation in curriculum. Over the years Beloit has stressed the values of individual concern and growth, reliance on the student's desire to learn, flexibility in the process of that learning, and a rigorous academic program. Experiential education and internationalism have been integral components of the liberal arts emphasis of the College. Approximately 1125 students are enrolled.

Paul J. Dovre, President
Concordia College–Moorhead
Moorhead, MN 56560

Paul Dovre received a B.A. from Concordia and Masters and Ph.D. degrees from Northwestern University. He has led Concordia College since 1975. Previously he served the College as a faculty member and academic vice president after a period of time when he was a faculty member at Northwestern. President Dovre has published in his academic specialty of speech communication. He has been an officer in various professional organizations including the presidency of the Lutheran Educational Conference of North America. He also served as the first chair of the Council of College Presidents of the Evangelical Lutheran Church in America and has been recognized by the government of Norway for his work.

"The purpose of Concordia College is to influence the affairs of the world by sending into society thoughtful and informed men and women dedicated to the Christian life" according to materials published by the college. Founded by Norwegian Lutheran immigrants, Concordia was dedicated in 1891 ten years after the first settlers made their homes in the upper plains area. The College has maintained strong relationships with Lutheran congregations of the area and is owned and operated by the congregations of the Evangelical Lutheran Church in America in northern Minnesota, North Dakota, and Montana. As an institution of higher education, Concordia seeks to enable students to develop as thinking, feeling, ethical human beings, and emphasizes that service is possible only in a community where individuals are interdependent. Approximately 2900 students are enrolled.

Victor Stoltzfus, President
Goshen College
Goshen, IN 46526-4798

President Stoltzfus earned a B.A. in social science from Goshen College and a B.D. in Theology from Goshen College Biblical Seminary. He received a M.A. from Kent State University and a Ph.D. from Pennsylvania State University, both in Sociology. He has been President of Goshen since 1984. Prior to that time he served as a pastor, magazine editor, professor, and dean at various institutions. His publications have addressed issues in health, agriculture, energy conservation, and the adaptive continuity of Amish life. He has participated in grants from the National Science Foundation, Title III of the U.S. Department of Education, and CETA of Illinois.

Goshen College began in 1894 as the Elkhart (Indiana) Institute of Science, Industry, and the Arts, a private preparatory school. It is now owned by the Mennonite Church and resides in Goshen, Indiana. As a ministry of the Church, Goshen College seeks to integrate Christian values with educational and professional life. Compassion and service are emphasized throughout the curriculum which includes a required international component. Approximately 1100 students are enrolled.

Bill Williams, President
Grand Canyon University
3300 W. Camelback Rd.
Phoenix, AZ 85107

President Williams earned his B.S. degree in mathematics from Grand Canyon College, an M.S. in Education from Arizona State University, an M.A. in Mathematics from the University of Illinois, and an Ed.D. in Mathematics Education from Arizona State. Prior to becoming president of Grand Canyon he was Professor of Mathematics and Chair of the Department of Natural Sciences and Mathematics at the Col-

154

lege. Before entering higher education he was a high school mathematics teacher. His scholarly work has addressed various aspects of mathematics with publications in biological systems modeling. He has been a recipient of several National Science Foundation grants and has received awards for outstanding teaching.

Grand Canyon College was chartered in 1949 by the Baptist General Convention of Arizona and became Grand Canyon University in 1989. A liberal arts institution, it attempts to attract ". . . capable, ambitious, and moral people who can benefit from a college education with a Christian emphasis and who are motivated by ideals of service in various fields of human endeavor." The curriculum and extra-curricular opportunities emphasize spirituality, critical thinking, an international perspective, aesthetic values, good health, and an understanding of one's heritage. Christian ideals are important to the University and lay the foundation for many formal and informal activities. Approximately 1800 students are enrolled.

Martha E. Church, President
Hood College
Rosemont Avenue
Frederick, MD 21701

President Church earned her A.B. from Wellesley College, M.A. from the University of Pittsburgh, and Ph.D. from the University of Chicago. She has been president of Hood College since 1975. Prior to that she served as an Associate Executive Secretary for the Commission on Higher Education, Middle States association of Colleges and schools; Dean of Wilson College and Professor of Geography at various institutions. Her publications include works in the spatial organization of electric power, geography, and higher education administration. President Church has held leadership positions and board memberships in many state and national organizations including: the American Association for Higher Education, the

American Council on Education, the Medici Foundation, the Carnegie Foundation for the Advancement of Teaching, and the Education Commission of the States.

Founded in 1893, Hood College describes itself as a contemporary liberal arts college for women. Over 90% of the students are women, and more than 30% of the undergraduate population of approximately 1175 are over twenty-five years old. Hood serves as a lifelong learning center where students can examine, evaluate and plan their lives. As means to this end, they are encouraged to participate in governance and undertake experiences that combine academic instruction and off-campus opportunities. Hood's curriculum combines a liberal arts core with practical experience in every major.

John H. Jacobson, President
Hope College
Holland, MI 49423

President Jacobson earned a B.A. from Swarthmore College and M.A. and Ph.D. degrees from Yale. He assumed the presidency of Hope in 1987. Previously, he had been a faculty member and administrator at Florida Presbyterian College (Renamed Eckerd College in 1972) and Empire State College of the State University of New York. He was Acting President at Empire State twice during the 1980s before coming to Hope. President Jacobson's publications include a variety of contributions in philosophy and higher education. He has considerable international experience including Fulbright and Ford Grants to Asia and consultantships in West Africa. His affiliations include groups interested in philosophy, theology, athletics, and higher education.

Hope College was chartered in 1866, the successor to an academy and school founded by settlers from the Netherlands in 1851. Today the College is affiliated with the Reformed Church in America, a heritage in which ". . . students and teachers [are] vitally concerned with a relevant faith that changes lives and transforms society." Hope's reason for being is the individual student. The College seeks to develop each one as a competent, creative, and compassionate person and offers 37 major fields as means to achieving these ends. Approximately 2800 students are enrolled.

H. George Anderson, President
Luther College
Decorah, IA 52101-1045

President Anderson received his B.A. from Yale, and both the M.A. and Ph.D. from the University of Pennsylvania. He also earned B.D. and S.T.M. degrees from the Lutheran Theological Seminary at Philadelphia. He has served as President of Luther College since 1982. Prior to that time he was President, Director of Graduate Studies, and Professor of Lutheran Theological Southern Seminary. His publications include works on ecumenical movements, Christian fellowship, family, Lutheranism, and church history among other topics. His professional activities include Chairmanship of the Board for the Evangelical Luther Church in America Publishing House, membership on the board of the Lutheran Educational Conference, the Commission on Studies of the Lutheran World Federation, and the Management Committee of the Division of World Mission on Ecumenism.

Luther College was founded in 1859 by the Norwegian Evangelical Lutheran Church and moved to Decorah, Iowa, in 1862. Presently supported by the Evangelical Lutheran Church in America, Luther describes itself as a Christian college of the liberal arts. As an academic community it is committed to the liberal arts where such an education disciplines minds and develops whole persons. As a community of faith, Luther encourages a Christian vision of service which expects the entire community to deal reflectively with challenges facing humanity. Approximately 2200 students are enrolled.

Roland Dille, President
Moorhead State University
11th St., South
Moorhead, MN 56560-9980

President Dille earned both his B.A. and Ph.D. degrees in English from the University of Minnesota. Prior to assuming the presidency of Moorhead State University in 1968 he held teaching jobs in high school, the University of Minnesota, St. Olaf College, California Lutheran College, and Moorhead State. He was dean at Moorhead State from 1966 to 1968. During 1982 he served as Acting Chancellor of the Minnesota State University System. President Dille has been a member of the Commission on Minnesota's Future and of the Minnesota Humanities Commission. He was a member of the National Council for the Humanities. He is past chairman of the American Association of State Colleges and Universities. He has written numerous articles and reviews in the fields of English and education, and he has been a part of educational missions to many parts of the world. He is presently editor of the *Heritage Press*.

The history of Moorhead State University goes back to 1885 and the establishment of a normal school in Moorhead, Minnesota. In 1921 the school became Moorhead State Teachers College, authorized to offer a four year degree of Bachelor of Science in Education. In 1975 the Bachelor of Arts degree was added, in 1956 the official name became Moorhead State College, and in 1975 it became a university which now offers more than 90 programs and majors to approximately 8400 students. The dominant missions of the institution are to facilitate teaching and learning, encourage research and artistic expression, and serve as a resource for the application of knowledge to the people in its geographical area.

Orley R. Herron, President
National—Louis University
2840 Sheridan Road
Evanston, Illinois 60201

President Herron earned his bachelor's degree from Wheaton (Ill.) College and both his M.A. and Ph.D. from Michigan State. Prior to assuming the presidency of National College of Education in 1977 he served as president of Greenville College, assistant to the president of Indiana State University at Terre Haute, and director of the doctoral program in student personnel work at the University of Mississippi. Earlier he held positions as dean of students, head resident advisor, and football coach. President Herron has authored five books and many articles regarding various aspects of education. He is a member of numerous boards and commissions including The Chicago Foundation for Education, The Foundation for Excellence in Teaching, Corporate/Community Schools of America, and the President's Council for the National Association of Intercollegiate Athletics.

The predecessor of National College of Education was a kindergarten and elementary school college founded in 1886. On June 9, 1990, at its 104th commencement, National College of Education became National—Louis University. Today the institution serves more than 13,000 students in various places: three campuses in Evanston, Chicago, and Lombard, Illinois; six academic centers including one in West Germany; and more than 40 extension sites in Illinois, Wisconsin, Missouri, Virginia, and Florida. The university has two colleges, education and arts and sciences.

David G. Horner, President
North Park College & Theological Seminary
3225 W. Foster Ave.
Chicago, IL 60625

President Horner received his B.A. degree in philosophy from Barrington College, a M. A. in philosophy from the University of Rhode Island, a M.B.A. from the Graduate School of Business at Stanford, and a Ph.D. from the School of Education at Stanford. Prior to coming to North Park in 1987 he held a variety of academic and business positions. He was President of Barrington College for six years starting in 1979. Dr. Horner has taught in the areas of business policy, business ethics, and the management of educational institutions. Currently he teaches both at North Park and at the Harvard Graduate School of Education. He serves on the boards of several schools and colleges and is a member of the President's Advisory Council for the Evangelical roundtable at Eastern college.

North Park describes its physical presence as "a small college in a great metropolis." Approximately 1100 students are presently enrolled. Founded in 1891 by first-generation Swedish-Americans, North Park is affiliated with and supported by the Evangelical Covenant Church. The College believes that a liberal arts education should prepare students for a rich, morally responsible life and equip them with those intellectual and social skills necessary to succeed in any vocation or pursuit. At North Park intellectual understanding is considered fragmentary unless ultimately joined to an understanding of one's spiritual nature. This "wholeness" of vision is supported by the curriculum as well as by community activities away from the campus.

John B. Slaughter, President
Occidental College
1600 Campus Road
Los Angeles, California 90041

John Slaughter began his collegiate education at Washburn University in Topeka and completed his baccalaureate in electrical engineering at Kansas State University. He later earned a M.S. in Engineering at UCLA and a Ph.D. in Engineering Science at the University of California (San Diego). He became President of Occidental in 1988. Prior to that time he was Chancellor of the University of Maryland, Director of the National Science Foundation, and Academic Vice President and Provost at Washington State University. He also has been a scientist in academic settings and in laboratories not directly linked to academia. President Slaughter's research specialty is in the field of digital control systems theory and applications. He is a co-editor of the International Journal on Computers and Electrical Engineering. In addition to positions in science and higher education he has been president of the Board of Directors of the San Diego Urban League, Chair of the Governor's Task Force on Teen Pregnancy for the State of Maryland, and Chair of the Prince George's County, Maryland, Public Schools Community Advisory Council on Magnet and Compensatory Education.

Occidental College was founded in 1887 by a group of Presbyterians but presently describes itself as an independent, coeducational college of the liberal arts. From 1958 to 1973 the College conducted a doctoral program in two areas of literature. It was discontinued to allow greater focus on undergraduate teaching. Occidental is committed to a philosophy of "total education." Intellect is considered a dominant component in a process which includes personal, ethical, social and political growth. Since 1963 the College has operated under a three course/three term academic calendar which stresses the opportunity for individual study and reading.

Bob R. Agee, President
Oklahoma Baptist University
500 W. University
Shawnee, OK 74901

President Agee earned his B. A. degree from Union University, both M.Div. and D.Min. from Southern Baptist Theological seminary, and a Ph.D. from the George Peabody College for Teachers of Vanderbilt. He became president of Oklahoma Baptist University in 1982. Prior to that time he served as Special Assistant to the President for Planning and as Vice President for Religious Affairs and Professor of Applied Ministry at Union. He also was pastor of churches in Tennessee and Kentucky. Dr. Agee has published works on higher education planning, selecting trustees, faculty development, and Biblical Studies. He is a member of the Board of Directors for the National Association of Independent Colleges and Universities, Vice Chairman of the Oklahoma Association of Independent Colleges and Universities, Chairman of the Education Commission of the Southern Baptist Convention, and a member of the Education and Evangelism Committee of the Baptist World Alliance. He also is a member of the task Force on Education and Economic Development for the Oklahoma state Chamber of Commerce and Industry.

Oklahoma Baptist University has its roots in the institution called Oklahoma Baptist College which dates back to 1889, but the University's "real founding" occurred in 1906. Owned and supported by the Baptist general convention of Oklahoma, the University acknowledges its Christian foundations and principles as it conducts educational programs in the arts, sciences, and other disciplines. This mission finds expression through a liberal arts core curriculum designed to prepare students for leadership and service, and through activities planned to stimulate spiritual, intellectual, social, cultural and physical development. Approximately 2000 students are enrolled.

P. Michael Timpane, President
Teachers College, Columbia University
525 W. 120th St.
New York, NY 10027

President Timpane received his B.A. in History and Economics and his M.A. in History from Catholic University. He also earned a M.P.A. from Harvard. He assumed his present position at Teachers College in 1984 following a period as Dean. Previously, he consulted for the Carnegie corporation of New York and worked in various roles for the National Institute of Education culminating in two years as Director. He has been employed by the Rand Corporation, Brookings Institution, and the United States Department of Health, Education, and Welfare. His publications in education have addressed communities of teaching, business and the public schools; politics of educational research; federal aid to education; and experimental schools.

Teachers College was founded in 1887 and became a part of Columbia University eleven years later. The faculty of Teachers College is designated as a faculty of the University, but the College retains its legal and financial independence. A graduate school, Teachers College is dedicated to "the systematic advancement of the sciences and arts associated with the educating, psychological, and health service professions." Flexibility in program planning and wide individual choice are available to students. The College emphasizes close faculty-student relationships combined with off-campus consultation and field research. Approximately 1500 full time and 4000 part time students are enrolled.

LB2165 .V54 1990   c.1
                       100106   000
A View from the top liberal

3 9310 00087657 1
GOSHEN COLLEGE-GOOD LIBRARY